PICTURES OF INITIATION
IN GREEK MYTHOLOGY

LEO HEIRMAN

PICTURES OF INITIATION
IN GREEK MYTHOLOGY

Illustrated
by
Charles Andrade

Franklin J Keune

April '91

SCHAUMBURG PUBLICATIONS, INC.
ROSELLE, ILLINOIS 60193

Library of Congress Cataloging-in-Publication Data

Heirman, Leo, 1914-1983.
  Pictures of initiation in Greek mythology.

Bibliography: p.
  Includes index.
  1. Mythology, Greek.   2. Anthroposophy.   I. Title.
BL782.H44   1987   292'.13   86-31642
ISBN 0-935690-03-4

iv

CONTENTS

ILLUSTRATIONS

FOREWORD

While preparing Leo Heirman's manuscript on Greek mythology for publication, we felt strongly that the text should be illustrated. But how? The answer should be simple. Greek mythology talks about places: Ephesus, Delphi, Athens, Thessaly, Crete, names still on maps today. Why not include landscape photographs and a map of the area where the voyages were said to have taken place? Right? Wrong!

When consulted, Leo Heirman, then still in retirement in the Netherlands, wrote saying that photographs would be incompatible with the atmosphere of the book. "Because in my view myths have nothing to do with time or space; they do not take place in the physical world, but in landscapes of the soul. Myths depict man's soul development. The fact that stories in this book stem from the Greek tradition is not at all essential to them. One could make a similar book of Icelandic mythology."

At that point we began to realize that we could no more project our modern thinking into people living thousands of years ago than they could have projected themselves, with accuracy, into our 20th century lives. Herein, we believe, lies the significant contribution of Leo Heirman's writing. With simple narrative language and vivid examples, he illustrates the differences between then and today, their selves and ours. He shows, for instance, in the way individual heroes met their trials—in Achilles' intense experience of self during periods of rage and in Hercules' struggle to overcome his instincts—the gradual development toward an increasingly sovereign intellect, such as we see evolving in Odysseus. The stories of archetypal heroes mirror not only the development of an individual, but also the inner form of Western civilization. Thus, it matters little whether a person by name of Hercules really lived, for he represents a type, an archetype; and it matters not at all whether we can physically retrace the wanderings of Odysseus, challenging as that may be.

As to illustrations, we hope Charles Andrade's sketches portray what Leo Heirman intended with his words. As Donald Bufano, a

Waldorf School teacher who studied with Heirman, writes: "Leo Heirman was a master of the story. Since his death in 1983, his art and understanding of story telling and interpretation live on in those who heard him and were taught by him."

May this also be true for those who read this book.

Ed.

PREFACE

This book is meant for parents, teachers, students, and all others who have pleasant memories of the Greek myths they heard or read when young and who would like to look at them again, perhaps to understand what caused these stories to seem so special. Children do not feel the need for such understanding; they take the myths, together with everything else in their lives, at face value; that is, as quaint, dramatic, entertaining stories. As adults, however, we may sense that myths contain more than meets the eye or ear.

Why should myths have more levels of meaning than merely the narration of divine deeds and heroic adventures set in ancient Greece? Are they symbolic? Did the storytellers seek to convey hidden lessons to their fellow men? Not likely. While the intention to moralize is obvious in Aesop's fables, it is absent in myths. Nor do myths symbolize another reality. The multiplicity of content that myths present is due to their having been produced in the days when an "old-fashioned" manner of thinking held sway, a type of thinking endowed with qualities different from ours. The thoughts of ancient peoples were less sharply focused, but had a broader, more subtly differentiated scope than our modern linear thinking, which tends to stride from abstraction to abstraction.

What is called the interpretation of myths is, properly speaking, more in the nature of a translation. For we need to translate the poetic and dramatic verbal images, in which early pictorial thinking was expressed, into the kinds of words that denote the clear, prosaic abstractions of our own intellectual thinking.

As G. S. Kirk indicates in *The Nature of Greek Myths*,[1] such interpretations can be undertaken from many different directions and points of view. The situation can be likened to giving a photographic "translation" of a sculpture in the round. Camera in hand, one can circle a statue, taking pictures from many different

1. G. S. Kirk, *The Nature of Greek Myths* (Baltimore: Penguin Books, 1974).

angles. When the photographs are developed, the statue will have been translated into, say, twelve different points of view, each of which will have its own validity. A survey of any number of such partial observations does not, however, lead to an experience comparable to the total experience of the statue in the round. To accomplish this, the points of view will have to be arranged organically.

It would be better to select just those pictures suggestive of the statue's character and the sculptor's intention and leave the others to specialists, such as professional sculptors and photographers, to study.

The fact that the myths have survived for more than two millennia indicates that they continue to provide something interesting, perhaps even inspiring, for readers and listeners. The fact that members of our technological culture are able to feel through images the importance of ancient myths suggests that it still must be possible to have a direct rapport with pictorial thinking, unscientific as it may be, and that it could well be possible, even for those of us who are no longer children, to learn this artistic thinking anew.

To understand this ancient pictorial thinking, one should not forget that the original versions of the surviving myths did not belong to what is called "literature." The artistic shape in which they have come down to us, fragmented, dramatized, and polished by the great authors and playwrights, is far removed from what was first given in the oral tradition. Prehistoric folktales were not written, but existed in the powerful memories of professional and amateur storytellers. These storytellers chanted in an inspired manner, thinking in pictures instead of in abstractions, not only when telling stories, but also when speaking.

Pictorial thinking is saturated with feelings. It represents a stage in the development of human thinking that preceded our modern, Western, adult manner of thinking in abstractions, in which we strive to be "objective." This earlier, pictorial state is normal for young children, as it was for our ancestors, who experienced their "childhood" in the so-called Hellenic Middle Ages.

The ancient Greek writers Homer, Hesiod, Aeschylus, and Sophocles revered the tales with which they had grown up and did not willfully alter the myths for the sake of their own dramatic intentions. It is, therefore, possible to reconstruct the original oral stories with some confidence as many mythologists have done.

One of the best of these is Edith Hamilton, who, in each chapter of her *Mythology*[2] marshals a treasury of ancient source material, which she blends into continuous narrations, pruning here and there to balance her nicely romantic reconstructions.

The ancient myths appeal to us, especially when we are young, because they depict human development towards the ideals of individual freedom and the overcoming of materialism. It is on this postulate that the author bases the interpretations in this book. Myths also depict at least twelve other aspects of the human situation. In the introduction and in the chapters that follow different aspects of this postulate will be elaborated, together with other principles of mythopoetic thinking.

The author's approach to the interpretation of myths owes a great debt to the works of Rudolf Steiner (1861-1925), and especially to the ideas set forth in Steiner's book *Christianity as Mystical Fact and the Mysteries of Antiquity.*[3]

After the introductory chapter there follow two chapters concerning the mythic gods; one about the creation and the hierarchies, and one about the children of Demeter. The following six chapters tell of heroes, of Perseus, Oedipus, Hercules, Jason, Theseus and, rather extensively, of Odysseus. The myths are retold in abbreviated form, with care to add here and there a sprinkling of some less well-known details, many of which can be found in Robert Graves' *The Greek Myths.*[4] At intervals the narration is interrupted to insert interpretations which owe a great debt to Frederick Hiebel's *The Gospel of Hellas.*[5] So that certain unusual ideas can be presented in more than one aspect, substantial repetition occurs in these commentaries. The number of notes has been kept to a minimum and a bibliography is given at the end of the book.

2. Edith Hamilton, *Mythology* (New York: New American Library, 1940).

3. Rudolf Steiner, *Christianity as Mystical Fact and the Mysteries of Antiquity* (Blauvelt, N.Y.: Rudolf Steiner Publications, 1972).

4. Robert Graves, *The Greek Myths*, 2 vols. (Baltimore: Penguin Books, 1955).

5. Frederick Hiebel, *The Gospel of Hellas* (New York: Anthroposophic Press, 1949).

INTRODUCTION

Nature is full of wisdom, full of the most intricate structures and processes working together as if in accordance with blueprints and plans. There are three ways in which we can come into contact with nature's wisdom: by studying it scientifically, by experiencing it with feelings of awe and reverence, and through technical applications. The reality of nature's innumerable forces and the wisdom in which they operate can be found within all earthly beings and things. In their manner of being, and in their manner of moving and growing, all natural processes participate in these forces. In human beings, and probably also in animals, this participation is indistinctly experienced as a feeling of being at home in the world, of having a sense of familiarity with one's environment. These feelings can be strengthened by physically moving and working within and in accordance with nature. The stronger man's active, willing participation in nature, the more self-evident becomes his overall feeling of well-being, and the less conscious he will be of what he is doing. Repeated actions lead to skills, which gradually become as "automatic" as a new set of acquired instincts. Reflection, on the other hand, be it on our participation in nature, on the feelings that it evokes in us, or on the skillful activities we perform within it, results in thoughts. Of our thoughts we are conscious; yet they have no more reality than reflections in a mirror.

While the forces of nature never stop working in our acts of will[2] and in our feelings, they do not penetrate our processes of thinking; instead, they are cast back and reflected by them. When

---

1. Rudolf Steiner, "Michaelmas" (Twenty-sixth Week), in *Calendar of the Soul* (London: Rudolf Steiner Press, 1963).

2. In the terminology of Rudolf Steiner's psychology, which we use here, the words "will" and "willing" do not indicate "desire"; neither do they mean "decision to act." Desire can be described as a feeling, decision as a thought, but the power or energy in our soul that makes us act, and that underlies and carries the motions of our limbs by which we perform our actions, we call will. Because this soul force is most deeply connected with the processes of the physical body, we are least conscious of it.

thinking, we remove ourselves from our unconscious participation in nature, and thereby become able to perceive nature. Thinking, by providing us with a quiet point of observation outside of and in opposition to nature, causes us to experience ourselves. We become conscious of ourselves as a subject vis-à-vis one or more objects, as a perceiver of something perceived, and as a detached and conscious thinker about that world with which we are unconsciously united.

Modern adult thinking manipulates abstract thoughts, a faculty children do not yet possess, but learn as they grow up. So, too, did the tribes of our ancestors during the developing stages of their cultures. In the course of Greek culture abstract thinking came into being with the ideas about nature that occurred to the Ionian philosophers. Such thinking took a great step forward with Anaxagoras; it was presented to the world by Socrates; and it was formulated by Aristotle, the systematizer of logic. It is not likely that the impact of the ancient philosophers on the everyday thinking of most Greeks was any stronger than the influence of modern philosophers is on us. In the next cultural period, at the end of the European Middle Ages, a similar transition to another mode of thinking took place, one which introduced the so-called Renaissance.

Before this gradual transition took place, people thought in a "medieval" way. Thinking was not yet an activity of their soul that could be carried on in isolation, abstracted, or more accurately, "extracted," from the totality of their soul life. Neither was it yet possible for them to produce visual art or music that had meaning in and of itself. Cultural life was a totality, and in all its parts and facets it was religious. Everywhere in nature there were perceived to be indwelling spirits; in plants, trees, and mountains, in water and in forests, beings existed that, in some aspects, ranked higher than man. The course of the year, the month and the week, were marked with religious celebrations. Artists depicted no other subjects than divine beings. No cultural environment exists in abstraction, but as the outward reflection of the collective life of a group of people who share a common way of thinking, feeling, and willing. "Mere" thinking did not yet exist. People did not consider it their intellectual duty to separate their feelings from their thinking, or to strive for objective, impersonal ideas. Just as children still do, they loved, hated, or were indifferent to what they thought. They also used more energy of will to fire their thinking activity, since they had to remember its results in detail, having not yet invented the use of writing.

The wisdom-filled activities which Mother Nature performs penetrate as motions the activities of humans and other beings. But in human thinking these activities present themselves in the form of images. Because the thinking of early Greeks was not yet abstract, but imbued with feelings, these images were full of color and fantasy. The people "in whom Nature spoke about herself" in such a pictorial way did not conceive themselves as individuals but as members of a family within a tribe and they took pride in contributing to the glory of family and tribe.

That such colorful thinking in images is characteristically tribal, i.e., nonpersonal, can still be seen in the languages we speak. Language, by its very nature, is social; otherwise, no member of the speech-producing community would be able to communicate with another. Modern languages are replete with imaginative expressions that still function pictorially, and always will. We commonly speak about the motions of inanimate things as if they were not merely matter but living, self-moving beings that really do something. We say, for example, the sun rises; the ball rolls, hits, bounces; the wheel turns; the motor runs; the clock ticks; the engine (she!) dies, etc. To indicate that inanimate things do not move from their places we also use action words, such as, a pillar stands, and so do the cups on the table and the trees in the forest. A remark can stand to reason; a car can sit in the driveway; some food sits or lies heavy in the stomach; a dress sits well on somebody. Our interest can lie before us; our life can lie in ruins. Deeds speak louder than words. Our company seized the opportunity, but it ran into difficulties. Fear sprang up in our hearts, however, we rose above it. Our life had a rendezvous with destiny, and so forth.

In modern technological times, languages quite often reverse the direction of their image making and speak about the human body as a machine that runs on sugar; about something by which a person is turned on or off; about some person who is instrumental in the acquisition of something. Love is often described as chemistry, methods as tools, moods as vibrations. It would not be difficult to collect many more examples of the abundant activity of image making that languages continually display.[3]

---

3. On its own level the genius of language displays the idea of Protagoras that "man is the measure of all things," by using the names of

Our thoughts in themselves, as well as the thoughts that make our feelings or actions known to us, have qualities such that they can be expressed in language. Therefore, some degree of kinship must exist between our silent thoughts and our audible words. What brings them together is the fact that the production of thoughts and the production of language both use images. The images modern people find in their thinking act as tokens or signs which label the products of thought so that they can be recalled when needed. The products of our thinking are never isolated, but interconnected through diverse associations. The relations between our thoughts are not, however, of our making; rather they are inherent in thought. They are qualities that guide our nonphysical thought activity, the concomitant physical movements of our nervous system, and its center, the brain, which we cannot perceive, no more than we can the activities of our will. One of the most important of these relations between abstract thoughts is the one between cause and effect: a causes b; b is the effect of a.

The images of early Greek thinking were much more dramatic, colorful, and clearly personified than modern abstractions. All motions or happenings in thinking were experienced as the actions of thought-beings. Cause and effect relationships appeared as the relation between parent and child. The visual quality of such thought images, their color, for instance, was more intense than in modern abstract thinking, in which the drive for clarity of form predominates. (An extreme caricature of a typical modern thinker would be that of a one-eyed, color-blind onlooker.) The sound qualities of thought images are vivid in both types of thinking. After all, in daily life thinking is basically an internal conversation with one's self. However, the knowledge of written letter forms, which in our time depict on paper the "real" words of our languages, tends to make our thought-words less "audible" and more abstract.

What modern people tell themselves when they are engaged in the activity of thinking can usually be written down as an article in a newspaper or scientific journal, or as a letter. In the majority of us, the inner language is apt to be full of cliches, which take the place

---

parts of the human body to indicate elements of clothing, implements, landscapes, etc. For instance: the head, foot, and sides of a table; the neck of a bottle, channel, shirt; the foot of a hill, ladder, list, page, wall; the mouth of a bag, cave, furnace, river; the tongue of a bell, buckle, scale, oboe; the shoulder of a road; the shoulder, lip, ear of a jug.

and save the trouble of thinking. In some of us, thinking will "jump the tracks" and we may speak poetry to ourselves. What early Greek people told themselves when engaged in the activity of thinking could be told aloud to others as colorful, dramatic, and poetic myths.[4]

A gifted teller of such myths, living dreamlike within the activities of the tribal group soul, able neither to read nor write, was at the same time a thinker of myths. And so were his fellowmen. Their thinking was pictorial. They were at home in their world, less distanced from it than we modern people, and they knew more about nature than we do. What they knew, they knew by contact, by looking, smelling, listening, touching, tasting, and through other hidden and less conscious activities of the senses. They could judge the age of an animal from a distance. They perceived which wild plants were good to eat, and which were poisonous. They "saw" what the weather would bring the next day[5] and they knew the time to plant certain crops by watching for the signal in the appearance of specific wildflowers. They knew what plants to use as medicine for man and animal by looking for their *signaturas*. They knew at what time a child or the young of an animal would be born by keeping track of the phases and position of the moon and the level of the tide in a nearby estuary. All this they learned through their practical, self-evident interest in the world they loved. They did not feel separated from nature, their mother, and therefore were not inclined, and were not even able to form abstract (i.e., separating) thoughts about her. People participated wholly within their environment.[6] Mountains and rocks were the bones of the living earth; rivers and seas its bloodstream; winds its breath; different vegetations signaled its moods. They felt how they belonged to the landscape in which they were born, and they loved it. This love was a form of religion, a feeling of belonging to all the divine beings that lived in streams, air, and soil. Their souls' major

---

4. The transition between the two ways of thinking is paralleled in the development of writing, which develops from pictograms, via hieroglyphs, into the abstract signs of the alphabet.

5. See Owen Barfield, *Saving the Appearances*, esp. chapter 11 "Medieval Environment" (London: Faber & Faber Ltd., 1957).

6. Learning still takes place through imitation, especially in young children. They imitate in motions every element of their environment, without first "thinking it out." This activity expresses their love for the world.

strength lay in its feelings; the strongest shaping force in social life was religion.

Myths are wisdom in pictures, the wisdom of Mother Nature, which penetrates man's limbs and lights up in the images of his thinking. Such beloved thought images could be easily remembered and could, therefore, be used in new combinations to express specific human conditions and conduct within the framework of nature, as the microcosm within the macrocosm.[7] Memory was aided by loving interest, which gave rise to many new inspirations. Greek mythology expresses this by conceiving memory as the goddess (Titaness) Mnemosyne, the mother of the nine Muses, the inspirators of the arts and sciences.

For the tellers of myths, language consisted of sounds for communication through audible expression.[8] The contents and, to a very great extent, also the form and the telling of the myths was part of an oral tradition. Preliterary people knew a great many stories, which especially gifted men, often blind, liked to tell, and which their audience enjoyed hearing. It is probable that in all the centuries, before the idea of writing occurred to somebody, certain developments and shifts of taste occurred, and that some ancient stories were popular in some decades and neglected in others. The total number of living myths would, therefore, fluctuate. Those stories survived which dealt with the general human condition, since they appealed to all audiences.

Man's power of memory was astoundingly strong in those days, as ours undoubtedly would still be if we did not allow ourselves the luxury of forgetting by writing things down. Because of the all-important role of memory, and the value placed on its veracity, stories were told with a musical voice in the form of ballads consisting of strictly metrical lines. Whatever the singer might

---

7. The human being is the small (micro) world within the large world (cosmos). Understanding the human being is the key to understanding the universe. This is the adult version of children's loving imitation of the world.

8. The style of life among preliterate people is sometimes called "acoustic." It is described by Marshall McLuhan as loaded with the strongest social (rather: tribal) interest, much more so than the social life of literate people who lead a "visual" life. This was already understood phenomenologically by Goethe when he considered the *signaturas* of both sense organs. The ear openings give access to the internal regions of the head; the eyes rest in bony sockets located on the surface of the skull.

forget in the course of his recitation had to be improvised in a form that precisely fit the lost number of syllables in the meter of the line. The number of possible replacements was therefore not very large. Professional storytellers soon began to invent and to collect stereotypic metric formulas which they could fit into different lines, either as an appropriate cliché or as an unspecific carrier wave. In this way, the singer kept the story going while he thought of his next line. Memory and invention, Mnemosyne and the Muses, went hand in hand.

Chanting epic lines is an organized and embellished manner of speaking based on a specific alternation of inbreathing and outbreathing. The greatest singer of tales, Homer, composed his epic lines as hexameters, a metre based on strictly organic rhythms. One is, therefore, justified in assuming that the singers who were not yet able to write used the same metre in their narrative songs, for which the Greek language, with its abundance of long and short vowels, was the natural medium.

Each hexameter consists of six ("hex") metrical units, or feet. In epic poetry such feet are traditionally dactyls, meaning "finger," of one long syllable, followed by two short ones. The two short syllables—because of the duration of their vowels—together take as much time to pronounce as one long syllable, which can also replace them. Such a replacement foot, consisting of two long syllables, called a spondee, is less lively than a dactyl and can at appropriate places be used to make the verse heavier, more encompassing, and more solemn. The mobility of the hexameter varies from 12 syllables, all spondees, to 17 syllables—all dactyls, except for the last one. Each verse begins strongly with a long sound, as if the singer were setting his foot down on solid ground. Then he takes two short steps, followed by a long one, followed by two short steps, completing two "feet." To avoid monotony, and also to take a breath, an interrupting silence, a caesura, occurs after the third long foot, which takes as much time as a spoken dactyl. At the very last instant of this silent foot, the singer takes a fast breath and continues with two short or one long syllable to complete the interrupted spoken foot. During this "silent dactyl," the last three syllables of his chant echo in him as an unspoken affirmation. The same happens at the end of the line. Graphically:

$$- \cdot \smile\smile \ . \ - \cdot \smile\smile \ . \ - \cdot \ (\smile\smile -) \ \smile\smile \ . \ - \cdot \smile\smile \ . \ - \cdot \smile\smile \ . \ - \cdot \ - \ . \ (- \ -)$$

Since the break does not fall at the end of the second, but within the third foot: not $- \smile\smile \ | \ - \smile\smile \ | \ -$, but $- \smile\smile \ | \ - \smile\smile \ | \ - \ | \ \smile\smile$, this silent echo of the last three syllables before the break does not sound like a normal dactyl, but like an inverted one, an anapest. This causes the rest of the verse often to be more anapestic than dactylic in metre, that is, to jump forward, rather than remain reflexive, and stately.

By no means is the hexameter a stiff marching 4/4 meter, but a dance in which dactyls, spondees, and anapests subtly alternate. When we write the metrical scheme down without bars, placing one part on top of the other, we see the following pattern:

$$- \cup\cup - \cup\cup -$$
$$\overline{\cup\cup} - \cup\cup - \cup\cup - -$$

The second part is similar to the first, but with a rhythmic prologue and epilogue. Each hexameter uses up two complete breathings: out/in out/in. Since in an adult the relation between breathing and heartbeat is 1:4, every dactyl, spoken or silent, is coupled to a heartbeat.

The recitation by memory was, therefore, not supported by a strong comprehensive faculty, diligently applied to memorizing the whole story, rather the singer knew his repertoire literally by heart. His performance was carried by the rhythmic system of his body with which, through unconscious imitation, the audience "walked in step," and in this way singer and audience were united. Since the majority of the listeners knew the poem by heart, their inaudible breathing and speaking along helped the singer remember. People attended the recitation of an epic poem not so much to learn an interesting story, but to enjoy, as a group, a performance of artistically spoken language. Such participation created a relaxed musical atmosphere and a form of dreamlike consciousness in which the wizardry of rhythmic and sound effects was enjoyed and the wisdom of the images appreciated.

Just as the thought content of myths rests on the soul's total involvement in the forces and rhythms of the world, so the telling of myths rests on the total involvement of man's rhythmic system in the metres of his chanted language. The cooperating rhythms of breathing and heartbeat are the physical vehicle of man's emotional life.[9]

9. In his psychological works, Rudolf Steiner describes our feelings as leading an oscillating existence between the poles of sympathy and antipathy. We automatically use as the instrument of our feelings the body's rhythmically oscillating processes centered in the chest. The knowledge we have of our feelings comes from thinking about them, but this knowledge is, of course, not the same as feelings themselves.

The colorful personages who make their appearances in myths had never lived in a certain place or at a certain time.[10] They have no dwelling place either in space or in history. Earlier audiences experienced them "within," that is, within the life of their souls. They are manifestations of the subtle and complicated forces of nature which, while at work in their bodies, were caught in the monitor of their thinking. All of nature's living forces are forces of growth, producing roots, leaves, or flowers, as well as the intricate structures of animals. Therefore, these forces appear reflected in our thinking as images of development and growth on various levels. In this respect myths have much in common with our dreams. They differ in being daydreams and are less egocentric than the ones we dream at night.

The most important figure in a myth is the hero in whom every listener sees himself. As the myth develops, we first hear about the circumstances of his birth, then of his life as a child, as an adolescent, as a mature person, and, lastly, of the circumstances that accompany his death. As long as the myth tells of the parents of the hero, we know that it speaks of his (and our) past. At the moment the hero enters upon the scene, we know that the myth is telling about us, ourselves.

Growing up, the hero usually lives a hidden life, in exile, out of reach of his father, that is, of any ancestral ideals or habits. When he reaches adulthood, the hero is ready to set out on his own and create a life as an individual. Most often he does not carry the name of his father's family. What is depicted as a father in a myth, in modern thinking would be described as the family tradition in which we grow up. For people living a tribal and not yet an individual life, the hero's development was felt to move in the direction of personal freedom, still a faraway ideal.

The necessary separation from ancestral influences is often depicted as painful and tragic, as illustrated in the myths of Oedipus and Perseus; sometimes the separation appears to be motivated by a need for safety, as with Hercules, Jason, and Theseus.

The period of his exile takes the hero away from the influence

---

10. In a myth the names of humans always have a meaning that characterizes them as types, instead of persons. Names of cities indicate the tribe in which the myth originated, rather than the geographical location where it was said to have taken place.

not only of his father, but also of his mother. Although his mother, too, belongs to an older generation, as an image, she has no connection with the hero's past. Not only because more often than not she is depicted as rather young, like, Danaë or Jocasta, but mainly because she belongs to a different family with a different name. When he leaves his mother, the young hero must learn a style of life and a set of habits other than those found at home in the bosom of family and tribe. The mother in us, who nurtures and protects us in traditional ways, is an image of tribal life.[11]

Breaking away from his father is practically always a definite step for the hero. In rare cases he makes a new connection with his past out of his own initiative, such as Jason and Theseus do. More often, the hero, on his way to the loneliness of a truly individual life, becomes afraid or tired and tries to go back into the safe tribal circumstances he left. This occurs in extreme form in the Oedipus myth, and more gently in the myth of Perseus.

When he comes out of exile, the hero has to stand many trials in which he must overcome all types of opponents, both human and animal. The course of his life generally takes place within land-scapes of known and unknown geography, across open seas, on remote islands, on mountains, and so forth, but in reality the journey occurs inside himself and reflects the course of an inner development. The beings he meets, be they friends, helpers, servants, competitors or attackers, human or animal, are all mythopoetic images of certain forces of his soul. Thus, every encounter leads to some degree of self-knowledge. The monsters and wild animals that seem to approach the hero are seen as in a mirror. They are the manifestations of his own instinctive powers streaming out from him. Sometimes he has to eliminate them, sometimes they have to be tamed. Our instincts are not in our consciousness; for that reason they appear in the image of animals. Meetings with human beings also show us images of ourselves, sometimes as grotesque caricatures of our lack of harmony,

---

11. The wisdom of the grandmother depicts tribal lore. (One can still see a vestige of this in Grimm's fairy tale "Little Red-Cap.") In modern languages, tribal as they still are, we find the words "father" and "mother" used in the senses indicated on this page. Coming from East or West, the immigrant left behind his "fatherland," the land of his ancestors, but did not want or dare to give up his "mother tongue" together with all the intimate social habits he or she was used to.

10

sometimes as an ideal to strive for. In contrast to our animal instincts, human beings depict attitudes and tendencies in our daily life of which we are unaware. Human images can be young, showing the freshness and vulnerability of a new trait developing in us, and they can be rich or poor, reflecting our wisdom or folly. Most importantly, they are either male or female. Men are images of our decision-making forces, women of our emotional life.

Becoming an individual, which is the ideal of growing up from both the tribal and the child's point of view, has to begin with detaching oneself from heredity (father) and environment (mother). Manifold processes of purification (often through fire or water), and of training (capturing and taming) have to be undergone and performed. Finally, the day will come in which the hero finds his spiritual ideal.[12] This ideal is nothing other than himself in his purely spiritual form. It is the real adult, the master of his instincts and willpower, at home in the stirrings of his soul, the one who makes himself responsible for his deeds, his thoughts, and the style of his biography. Man's spiritual form is the Unique One, who is able to call himself "I," after having found the way to distinguish between his real self and his pseudo-selves or his lower egos. In mythopoetic thinking this ideal spiritual self appears as the wonderful princess whom the hero marries. Union with one's spiritual self, after it was recognized, is also the aim of schooling

---

12. Since the words "spirit," "soul," and "body," will be used often, it is important to explain the meaning of these three terms in Rudolf Steiner's psychology, which is at the basis of our interpretations. My thoughts, my feelings, and those forces that underly my deeds, form the life of my soul in its three main components. This total soul life of mine is performed upon the instruments of my bodily organizations: thinking is performed on the physical and chemical happenings in the network of my nerves and brain; feeling on the vibrations of my rhythmic system; willing on the metabolic processes in the muscles of my limbs. We have to emphasize that my body and my soul are not independent; they are the body and the soul of ME. When this "me" speaks about itself, as a being in action, it calls itself "I." This "I" is essentially myself. It is not a part of my soul, but its master and owner. It is neither soul, nor body. It is spirit. This spiritual being finds its modes of existence in different states of consciousness. It is "awake" when confronting the images of thinking, "adream" while carried by the vibrations of feeling, "asleep" within the realities of doing. Steiner describes man not as twofold, but as threefold; as a spiritual being, equipped with both body and soul.

towards initiation. A wedding can, therefore, represent an initiation (which can be called a "mystical marriage").

Such a union can produce spiritual offspring, daughters, sons, or both. Just as the father depicts the hero's past and the mother his present, his children are images of his future, either of how he will be or how he hopes to become. Images of children are, after all, the hero's own production, or reproduction. A daughter represents his spiritually renewed emotional life. Still very tender and vulnerable in the beginning, she will grow to lead a life of great love and prudence. A son depicts the hero's spiritualized willpower. This can strengthen until the hero identifies with it as his renewed spiritual being. This accomplishment is a higher form of initiation. A frequent motif at the beginning of myths is the confusion and despair of a man, who, having wished for a son all his life, suddenly realizes that this renewed being of his, of necessity, must take his place and render obsolete his beloved and well-known old self.

There are many different ways to explain what myths have to say. The one applied in this book starts with the premise that human thinking itself is going through an evolution and that the original myth makers thought in pictures, rather than in abstractions. Explaining the myths, therefore, is tantamount to translating a language of images into a language of abstractions. Myths are wisdom in pictures, which tell the story of human growth toward individuality.

THE GREEK GODS AND THE CREATION

Hierarchies

We have learned to take Greek culture seriously and to admire the works of Greek philosophers, sculptors, architects, authors, and politicians. Strangely though, we make an exception for Greek religion, although it must have been the profoundest expression of Greek culture. The ancient Greeks worshipped many gods and goddesses, so many we hardly know what to think of all these "gods." To modern man, accustomed to the cultural traditions of the West, where all religions are monotheistic, the idea of a multitude of gods seems unreasonable and even irreverent. For us, the word "god" does not have a plural.[1] We might do better, therefore, to call the Greek gods spiritual beings.

In our own religious traditions we find that the divinity is not the only inhabitant of the nonphysical realm that we call heaven. Other heavenly beings, called angels and archangels, are thought to be able to influence man, although they do not live in a physical body. Traditionally, there are nine groups of such spiritual beings, all of different power and rank. They are called the nine hierarchies and all except for the two highest, which retained their Hebrew names, cherubim and seraphim, have Greek names. Often we find these nine "choirs of angels" divided into three larger hierarchies.

Although at the peak of Greek culture certain philosophers, such as Heraclitus and Plato, had penetrated to the idea of one god, the less educated people felt surrounded by hosts of spiritual beings whom they called gods. These Greek gods are the supersensible beings whom the Christian tradition calls archangels and angels.

For us, in our present form of consciousness, it is hardly possible to imagine a being that is without physical form, such as an archangel or a Greek god. It could be of help first to conceive of

---

1. However, we should not forget John, 10:34. "Ye are gods" (*Theoi este*).

13

such a being in the abstract as a presence. Then one might consider that the size—that is, the power of such a presence—should be shown larger than the human form—it could even loom taller than a skyscraper—and there is no reason to think of such beings as symmetrical. Imaginatively, one could approach the visualization of spiritual beings as invisible "flares," showing themselves as forces, rather than forms.

To the Greeks it was clear that their gods gave evidence of their presence in all that happened in nature. But in historical times the gods themselves could no longer be perceived by most people as beings. To "see" the invisible gods and to "hear" the nonphysical sounds of their voices, one had to live in a dreamlike consciousness saturated with religious feelings. This state of consciousness was no longer possible for people who, in their way of thinking, were growing apart from their environment, to the extent that they became capable of describing it objectively.

Earlier Greeks, those living around 1000 B.C., were not yet so far developed. They could neither read nor write, and they did not find themselves important as individuals. They were proud to be members of their tribe and, within it, of their clan and of their family. They lived their daily lives in shades of unclear conscious-ness which must have been like a permanent state of daydreaming, in which vague but strong emotions are more important than thoughts. This kind of thought life could not develop scientific or philosophical systems, but it did produce religion and myths. Such people's thoughts were not "objective," such that the logical links between causes and effects were apparent abstractly, but their thoughts were imprinted with strong, personal feelings. As a result, a cause and its effect appeared to them in the picture of parent and child, in their diverse relations.[2]

Mythical personages, animals, and landscapes moved as images through people's dreamlike thinking; instead of abstract thoughts, pictorial elements arose within them and with these images they grasped what they perceived in the world and in themselves.

---

2. A good example of such pictorial thinking can be found in the modern expression, "necessity is the mother of invention," which we, in a more or less playful, old-fashioned manner, sometimes use instead of the abstract statement, "because one needs something very much, one will work hard enough to find it."

Myths, even in the incomplete and dramatized forms in which they have survived in the works of the great writers, give the impression of being very ancient and mysterious. Long ago they could have originated in the following manner. In the course of their reflections on life, important picture thoughts would have arisen in priests and in minstrels. When such picture-thought processes were told as stories, their value was also understood by those listeners who themselves would not have been able to conceive such stories or thoughts. They became part of a growing body of tales and myths, faithfully preserved in oral tradition.

During this period, which may be called the Hellenic Middle Ages, a substantial number of clairvoyants, people who had a pictorial awareness of their reactions to the presence of non-physical beings and actions, must still have lived among the members of the tribe. We have no proof of this in Greek culture, but clairvoyants are known to have existed among people who lived in a similar state of consciousness in Iceland around 1000 A.D. Irish monks, who had come north to Christianize them, reported that many pagans could perceive what they called each other's "follow-angel."

Out of the cosmogonic myths it can be understood that in still older forms of consciousness people were completely united with nature in their inner and outer experiences and activities. People partaking in this primordial form of inner life are described in mythical stories as being in a state of paradise, a state in which man was unselfconsciously in total contact and participation with the hierarchies and their creative workings. The paradise story at the beginning of the Old Testament gives a clear picture of this original situation as it appeared to Hebrew mythopoetic thinking.

Religion, both in its inner form of love and reverence for the gods and as expressed in rituals and myths, is the source of all culture. At the end of the Middle Ages, science, based on objective thinking, and art, the product of skillful doing, were gradually extracted from the realm of religion, which is essentially born out of human feelings. As scientific thinking evolved, awareness of the gods receded.[3] However, even in later Greek culture, when philosophic thinking flourished and people began experiencing themselves as individuals, there were still ways for some of them to

---

3. Since Richard Wagner, this state is called "*Die Götterdämmerung*," i.e., "the twilight," or rather, "the dimming of the gods."

come into direct contact with the gods in the supersensible spiritual world. This was possible for those who reached the state of initiation after a rigorous and prolonged training of the soul in spirit sensitivity. Such training took place in mystery schools, of which the best known were located on the island of Samothrace, in Eleusis, and near Ephesus.

In addition, there was a way for all people to approach certain gods in an indirect manner. In places called oracles,[4] the gods spoke in unfamiliar tongues through the mouth of a medium who, in an induced state of trance, muttered or shrieked sequences of sounds. These were then interpreted and translated into Greek verses by the attending priest. In this form, the oracle's utterances became the god's answer to the question asked by the pilgrim. The most important oracle was the one at Delphi, in the center of Greece, where a female medium, called the Pythia, was Apollo's mouthpiece. An older oracle was the one at Dodona in the northern mountains. Here three old priestesses, called the Doves, interpreted the moaning of the wind in a creaking oak tree as pronouncements coming from Zeus, the oak tree being sacred to Zeus.

The nine choirs of angels—the word angels is here used in a generic sense—or the nine hierarchies, which are still mentioned sequentially in the ritual of the Roman Catholic mass, appear within Greek religious thinking in three groups of three, represented as generations of gods. The first gods who worked upon the developing world in its oldest stages prepared the way for a younger family of gods who organized a second stage of world evolution. When the influence of this second hierarchy had waned, a third hierarchy, that of the archai, archangeloi, and angeloi came forward as the Olympian gods. In each case, the youngest representative of the hierarchy became the leader of the new stage of development. In the cosmogonic myths these transitions are depicted as battles in which the youngest son and his brothers succeed in overthrowing their father and his generation.

Greek Myths of Creation

The gods whom the Greeks primarily worshipped were the

---

4. The Latin word *oraculum* means "mouthpiece."

Olympians: the three divine brothers Zeus, Poseidon, and Hades, together with their sisters Hera, Demeter, and Hestia. Zeus, the youngest of the group (Poseidon is the eldest), was considered to be the father of gods and men. Around these six great gods (archangels) we meet many divine children of Zeus, such as the goddesses Artemis, Aphrodite, Athena, and Hebe, and the gods Apollo, Ares, Hephaestus, and Hermes.

Religious people felt, and myths told them, that in earlier, prehistoric times there must have been an older generation of gods who, when no longer able to keep up with earthly evolution and with human culture, had been overthrown by the Olympians. These earlier, obsolete gods were the gigantic Titans, the youngest of whom, Cronus, was the father of the six Olympians, the gods of heaven and earth. Other Titans had been the parents of stellar gods, such as Eos (the dawn), Helios (the sun), and Selene (the moon). The Titans Iapetus and Themis became the parents of Prometheus and his brothers. The Titaness Mnemosyne (memory) was the mother of the nine Muses, the forces of artistic inspiration.

Earlier, at the very beginning of creation, an older hierarchy, consisting of Gaea (earth) and Uranus (heaven) first parented monsters and giants, and later produced the twelve mighty Titans.

Still earlier, before heaven and earth existed, in the farthest reaches of time, the evolution of the world began with a great, structureless emptiness, called chaos (yawning). Out of chaos, after endless eons, arose Nyx, the depth of darkness, a female being, and her brother Erebus, the depth of death. A third being, the greatest creative force of all, was the great god Eros (longing). Eros everywhere acts as attraction, love, order, beauty, and light, and never will he become obsolete.

From the very beginning, Eros is at work in all wordly realms. His essence is longing. In the mineral realm he appears in the form of gravity and magnetism and is responsible for keeping all of Mother Earth's children with her. He is also active in relations between the sun and the plants, between male and female animals, and between humans. The Greek myths tell us that it was the influence of Eros on the primordial beings Nyx and Erebus that caused the next generation of gods to be born.

This generation, the first hierarchy, consists, as mentioned before, of the two beings, Uranus and Gaea, heaven and earth. Uranus represents all that is spiritual in the world; Gaea is the universal mother. Through the intervention of the Eros force they

17

become the parents of many giants. These, their first tentative offspring, became wild and terrifying monsters. At birth they were abducted by their father and imprisoned in the Tartarus, the deepest realm of the earth, twice as deep as Hades, the realm of the dead.

Later, Gaea gave birth to the majestic Titans, twelve mighty beings of great power and fierce beauty. As children of Uranus, the world spirit, they formed the creative nature of the living world. There was in them no clarity of contemplation, no versatility of feelings—only a constant gigantic stream of willpower. The out-flowing power of divine will manifested itself as the Titans' children, beings who lived in nature, creating and sustaining the natural world. Best known among them were the water spirits, the mountain spirits, and the tree spirits, together with the elemental beings. The earth was the physical embodiment of the Titans. The monsters placed in Tartarus became part of Mother Earth.[5]

The Titans formed the second hierarchy. The youngest of them, Cronus, helped his mother, Gaea, take revenge on his father, who had imprisoned Gaea's older children in the Tartarus. He emasculated Uranus, in this way bringing an end to the creative activities of the primordial world spirit. Then Cronus ruled in his father's place over all the beings of nature. However, he did not fulfill Gaea's wish. He left all her monstrous offspring safely where they were. Cronus, who wanted to prevent his own children from eventually deposing him, did the same as his father had done, but at an earlier stage. As soon as they were born, he swallowed them whole. They lived on within the nature of their father, waiting to be born again as adult gods. Only the youngest son, Zeus, was spared when his mother, Rhea, gave Cronus a wrapped-up stone to eat as a substitute.

Zeus, newly born, was taken to Crete, the large island, situated on the threshold of the Aegean Sea, and the seat of the pre-Greek

---

5. Twice the idea of reincarnation or rebirth makes a cautious appearance in the cosmogonic myths: once when Mother Earth, Gaea, had produced her first monster brood, and their father, Uranus, impris-oned them in the Tartarus, i.e., they were reabsorbed by their mother's body, out of which Zeus would set them free; and again when the children of Cronus and Rhea are reabsorbed by their father, to be reborn later by the action of Zeus.

Minoan culture.[6] In a cave in the side of Mount Ida on Crete, nymphs took care of the divine child. When grown, Zeus came to his father's palace as a stranger and put a magic substance into his father's wine, which made Cronus vomit up all his sons and daughters. Then war in heaven began to rage between the Titans and the younger gods, later called the Olympians. Although he made use of the advice of the great Prometheus, and was helped by the monsters from the Tartarus, it took Zeus and his hierarchy ten years to overcome the untamed forces of nature, the hierarchy of the Titans.

Next in importance to Cronus are the three brothers Atlas, Prometheus, and Epimetheus, sons of the Titan Iapetus. For his share in the war against the Olympians, Zeus punished Atlas by appointing him permanently to bear the vault of heaven. Prometheus allied himself with the future, with the young Olympians in the heavenly war against the Titans, and acted as an advisor to Zeus. On his suggestion, Zeus freed the monsters in the Tartarus so they could help in the struggle against Cronus. To show their gratitude, the gigantic beings forged battle gifts for the gods. Zeus received from them his dreaded thunderbolt, Hades his helmet of invisibility, Poseidon his sharp and shining trident. With these weapons, and with the enthusiastic help of the raging monsters, the gods overcame the Titans. Again on Prometheus' advice, Zeus imprisoned the defeated Titans in Tartarus. The creative powers under the earth, or microcosmically, the powers of will deep in us, are never illuminated by the sun of our consciousness.

Next, the Olympians, the third hierarchy, divided the organization of the world. Zeus was given rule of the sunlit air. Externally, he is the "sky father" who brings order into the world and protects those who travel in it; internally, Zeus enlightens man's consciousness. Poseidon is the regent of the water element and works within the life processes of man's body. Hades rules the mineral earth, imprisoning man within the weight of his physical body. He also receives the souls of the dead within his dark realm. Hera preserves all cultural traditions and is the goddess of marriage. Hestia cultivates family and social life, which in the homes of ancient peoples centered around the hearth. Demeter lives with everlasting care within the world of plants, both wild and cultivated.

6. Having their father god, Zeus, grow up on Crete, shows that the Greek tradition considered the Minoan culture to be the prehistoric introduction, or childhood, of their own culture.

Most other Olympians are children of Zeus, and each has a particular task to perform. Athena, the goddess of Athens, who was born out of her father's head, presides over divine and human thinking, over wisdom and inventiveness. In many myths, Athena, a virgin goddess, plays a role as the hero's adviser and the inspirator of his ideas.

Hermes, who is equipped with wings on his round hat and on his golden sandals, is the herald of both Zeus and Hades. Swift like the wind, he is busy the whole day as a messenger flying everywhere within the upper as well as the lower world. Present in the agility of man's power of will, Hermes often works together with the wise goddess Athena.

Apollo, the enemy of barbarism, gradually becomes the tribal god of the Greeks. He speaks through his mediumistic priestess, the Pythia, to those who ask advice from his oracle at Delphi. Aided by the nine Muses, he is active in all the sciences and arts of the Greeks. He is a dragon killer with bow and arrow, a musician with stringed instruments, and a healer. He is also worshiped as the shining countenance of the sun.

Artemis, Apollo's sister, called the Maiden of the Silver Bow, is a moon goddess and a huntress in the mountains. Her tasks are many and she appears under different names.

Hephaestus fell from heaven and was born lame and ugly. On earth, he inaugurated the difficult and magic art of metalworking in gold, bronze, and iron. He is the Greek god of fire, that most powerful and least physical of the four elements.

Aphrodite, originally the Great Goddess or Great Mother, the powerful goddess of fertility in the Aegean area, became goddess of physical love when Greek invaders adopted her. She was married to Hephaestus, but preferred Ares, the god of war.

But nobody, not even Aphrodite, really loved Ares, the god of brutish warfare. Hebe, the goddess of youth, is the cupbearer of the gods who became the wife of the hero and half god Hercules after his assumption to Olympus.

The Human Beings and Their Fate

Prometheus, a friend and helper of Zeus, is essentially a Titan, and represents the forces of creation, development, and will. Although men were already present on earth during the reigns of the older

CHARLES ANDRADE
87

hierarchies, they did not yet live like human beings. Prometheus had great interest in these early beings and wanted to foster their development; another tradition even considers him their actual creator. Knowing in advance the fateful consequences, Prometheus, out of his own free will, stole from heaven a spark of the gods' divine fire for man's behalf. He carried the spiritual fire down to earth concealed in the slow-burning pith of a fennel plant. With this gift mankind was able to develop the arts of civilization, all of which directly or indirectly are built on the mastery of fire.

Strengthened and inspired by the divine fire that now worked in them, people began a cultural development that made them less and less dependent on the gods. To punish Prometheus and mankind for this deed and its consequences, Zeus commanded the fire god Hephaestus to create the first woman. As her name, Pandora, indicates, she was a wonderful creature, endowed with all the gifts of the gods. Zeus sent her to earth, carrying in a jar additional gifts for man, and gave her as a present to Epimetheus who, in spite of his brother's warning, accepted the gift. When, out of curiosity, she opened the jar, all the plagues and miseries flew out to forever roam the world of men. This was man's punishment, the price of his independence. Hope, the only good gift of the gods was left at the bottom of the jar.

The Myth of Prometheus

As punishment for stealing the gods' fire, Prometheus was led by Hephaestus to the eastern edge of the known world, to the Caucasus mountains between the Black and the Caspian Seas. There, he was chained with his back to a rock, unable to move. Every morning a vulture descended to gnaw his liver, which grew back every night. His great suffering was to last until a being voluntarily gave up his life for him in the company of a hero who would come to set him free. However, at the time of Prometheus' imprisonment, the hero had not yet been born.

With great courage and patience, Prometheus, the friend of man, endured his punishment, caused not only by Zeus' anger, but also by his fear. From his mother, the Titaness Themis, Prometheus had learned an important secret: Zeus, like his father Cronus, and his grandfather Uranus before him, would be replaced by one of his future sons if he refused to marry the mortal woman who would give birth to his child. Themis told Prometheus that after a very long time the great hero Hercules would come to the Caucasus in the course of performing one of his twelve labors. Out of pity and compassion he would kill the voracious vulture. When the time finally came, the wise centaur Chiron, who suffered from an incurable wound, came the long distance to the Caucasus with Hercules. In exchange for the freedom of Prometheus, Chiron sacrificed his immortality; then Hercules was allowed to kill the vulture and set Prometheus free. From then on, Prometheus was again a friend of the gods.

To understand this important myth in relation to man's fate it is necessary to translate the sequence of images into concepts. Prometheus belonged to two worlds. He was closely connected with the Olympian gods, but, as a Titan, he was also a being of creative will. He took upon himself to be the supporter and representative of mankind. Thus his fate became the fate of man, in whose soul he had caused a divine spark to burn and shine.

When the end came to the era called by the Greek storytellers the Golden Age, or, as told in the Old Testament, when Adam and Eve, through their developing knowledge caused themselves to be expelled from Paradise, man (Prometheus) began living in a state of being in which he was chained to his physical body (the rock) within the physical world. Throughout this painful transition, suffered in a loneliness of his own making, he consoled himself with the knowledge of a great secret. Prometheus knew that the spiritual principle (Zeus) had to unite itself with man's mortal being, the body-bound soul, depicted as a mortal woman, to bring forth a new, spiritual man—the divine son. The spiritual in man would then take the place of the guiding principle, which up to that point in human development had acted externally. Prometheus (the human being) was not free to betray this secret until an initiate, the hero Hercules, had traveled all the way to find him. By force of his initiation, Hercules would be able to eliminate the body-bound consciousness of daytime (the predatory bird), which through the insatiable greed of its senses destroys the healthy forces in man's living body (the liver).

The sensory system of man often appears in myths in the image of a keen-eyed, never resting, predatory bird. The activities of our senses (bird), while we are awake (morning), prey upon the vegetative growth of our living processes, which has its strength restored during sleep, i.e., in the absence of consciousness. The

liver, the largest metabolic gland, appears as an image of our life forces. When the greed of the senses has been overcome, the human being can be delivered by sacrificing the centaur in him, his half-human, half-animal being. The instinctive or centauric part of man (Chiron), must die in order to free his creative spirit (Prometheus), a process which takes place in some people at the moment of initiation, in all others at death. The secret that mother Themis (she who knows the rules) told her son, that out of the transitory (the mortal woman) the eternal (the divine child) will be born, lives in man's soul in the form of the hope that sustains Prometheus. His brother, Epimetheus, (he who reflects upon [epi] what has past and is transitory) acquires all suffering and misery, the gifts of Pandora. Prometheus (he who thinks forward [pro] creatively) rejects the transitory. Zeus and the Olympian gods will be dethroned in people's consciousness, a gradual process known as "the dimming of the gods." Human beings, however, have acquired the divine spark within. Without the aid of the external gods they will be guided by themselves, i.e., by the spiritual being (the divine son, Dionysus) who lives in everyone's soul.

THE CHILDREN OF DEMETER

Persephone Expelled From Paradise

The great Olympian goddess Demeter, the force of growth in all plants and trees, had a most lovely daughter, called Persephone. When this daughter grew up, she was kidnapped by Hades, the dark god of the realm of the dead, and married to him. Blinded by her sorrow, the divine mother ceased to take care of her domain and everywhere the earth began to die. When Zeus saw this, he persuaded his brother Hades to give up his young bride for one half of each year. From then on, in the sunshine of spring and summer, Persephone lives with her mother on the surface of the earth, rejoicing in the wonderful shapes and colors of the plants about her, and in the strength of their healthy growing. In autumn and winter, Hades has her back in his dark kingdom under the earth, a time when most plants have fulfilled their lives and only the seeds and the roots are living underground.

On the surface, this sounds like a nature myth, a type of story comparatively rare in Greek mythology. Mother Nature's beloved daughter, the essence of her being, is working on earth in the plants when they are growing, and disappears below in winter to keep the seeds alive. Undoubtedly, the behavior of the earth's vegetation could have been dramatically depicted in such a myth. Apart from the fact that some details (such as the forceful kidnapping, and the much too deep and stony characterization of Hades' realm) are hard to fit into a nature myth, there is much more to the story of Persephone.

In the first place, there is no need for Persephone, a goddess, to work in the garden of earth, since her mother, Demeter, has all the indwelling elemental beings at her command, and these little Titans are perfectly capable of caring for the seeds and roots. Second, her descent into the earth is preceded by a most interesting development that has nothing to do with vegetation. In addition, her life as queen of the netherworld, as it is spoken of in myths and hymns, has no bearing on any aspect of plant life in

winter, but rather personifies her as a cathartic power in the great mystery rituals of Eleusis.

The original creators of the Greek myths did not study nature's happenings with the intention of inventing pictorial stories to explain them. Rather, they experienced themselves in open contact with the world outside. What happened there in the "large world," the macrocosm, was at the same time taking place within their own bodily being, the "small world" or microcosm. The rhythmical yearly repetition of nature's processes showed them again and again in a timeless way what had occurred in their own development as human beings.

Within their own nature, which they called Demeter, they all felt Persephone as their soul daughter. Her story is a depiction of the fall of man's soul.

The idea of a god as father and nature as mother recurs in Greek mythology in an older hierarchy, in the relation between Uranus and Gaea at the beginning of the earth's development. This is repeated during the reign of the Olympians in the connection between the god Zeus, father of gods and men, and the goddess Demeter, mother of vegetation. Although his sister Hera was to become his actual spouse, the creative powers of Zeus were so great that he also had offspring by many other goddesses, as well as by mortal women. The latter he could never visit in his divine form, for they would not have survived his divine presence. To them he came in disguise, e.g., as a bull (to Europa), a swan (to Leda), a golden rain (to Danaë). In this myth, the offspring of the union of father god Zeus, and Mother Nature Demeter is the goddess Persephone. She is a creature of nature, begotten by the god of the heavens, the sky-father, and, therefore, a spiritual entity as well. In the myth of Prometheus we found the idea of man's double nature stated in an image of earthly men receiving from the Titan's son a spark of the heavenly fire. In the myth of Persephone, the human soul is depicted as the daughter of spirit and nature, Zeus and Demeter.

Persephone grows up in the continuous presence of her loving mother and with the blessing and love of her distant father in the heavens. Her mother, the great artist who creates nature's forms, teaches her to embroider upon a veil images of all that had happened in the past to the Olympian gods. In this way Persephone stays in contact with the Olympian world while on earth with her mother and learns how it was in the beginning, when her father

31

and his brothers were fighting the war in heaven. She learns that there was an abundance of terrible monsters all over creation, who helped the Olympians dethrone the hierarchy of the Titans. As Persephone matured, her mother began to worry, for every day she expected the god Eros, whom she had noticed in the neighborhood, to appear and bring confusion to the quiet youth of her daughter.

Eros, the enormously powerful, original god who made the world into an organized cosmos and, by inspiring longing and desire, caused so many living beings to come into the world, had some disturbing characteristics. Once when Demeter had to leave her daughter alone, to attend to her tasks in nature, she warned Persephone that she should be prepared for a visit from the wonderful god, eternally young and self-renewing, who would incite her to pick the flowers that were growing about. She cautioned Persephone not to listen to his words and not to stop her embroidery, so that her hands would always be busy. Demeter left in fear, with the intention of returning as quickly as possible, while her daughter sat sedately on the grass in the midst of the spring flowers, concentrating on her embroidery. She did not look up when Eros came, but when he sat next to her and spoke in a voice such as she had never before heard, she could not help listening. Soon her hands stopped doing their work and she gazed up at the handsome god whose enormous power she felt around her. Her embroidery, her connection with the past, was now interrupted. Confused, she sat idle. Not knowing what to do in the present, where she had never consciously been before, she looked for the first time at the beautiful flowers around her.

When Eros showed her how to break one off, and lovingly contemplate it close at hand, she followed suit, undoing her mother's work. Instantly, her whole idea of life changed. She stood up and walked across the meadow, involved in thoughts of her own and experiencing new emotions. She felt an overwhelming love for the beauty of the world and longed to become at home on earth. Eros disappeared. She felt unstable, and it was as if the earth rumbled. Suddenly, the meadow split open and a large black hole appeared. The sounds of horses, their breathing, the stamping of their hoofs, the tinkling of their harnesses arose out of the earth. Persephone stood rooted to the ground. Majestically, Hades arose out of the netherworld in his chariot led by black horses. He stretched out his arm, pulled her next to him and, without coming to a stop, the chariot descended into the earthly realm—an image signifying the fall of man's soul.

The story of the fall of man's soul is best known in Western culture through the first book of the Old Testament. In Genesis human beings live in a state of paradise, with neither sickness nor death, and without having to labor. They enjoy open, uninterrupted contact with nature and a permanent orientation in response to the loving deeds of God the Father. The paradise story focuses on Eve, who, together with Adam, leads a sheltered existence in which they are sustained by the fruits of the tree of life. This life ends when Eve is visited by a snake hiding among the leaves of another important tree, the tree that gave man the knowledge of good and evil. The snake god speaks to her and entices her to eat from the tree of knowledge, promising that "your eyes will be opened, and you will be like God, knowing good and evil."[1]

In so doing, Eve and Adam wake up to maturity, become aware of their sexual nature, and for the first time enter the physical world. They now are condemned to suffer all the miseries inherent in living with a physical body in a physical environment, all "the gifts of Pandora," exemplified in the text by reference to bodily exhaustion and painful childbirth. At the same time, they are now able to perform deeds of their own volition and strive towards inner freedom. There is no reentry into paradise, the gates of which are guarded by beings of the highest hierarchies.

Every child, in growing up, experiences at the outset of adolescence expulsion from the paradise of childhood. Striving for independence, interest in the physical body, sexual drives, all come to development. Every individual, in growing up, repeats the development of the human race, about which mythologies tell us in dramatic images. When forced out of the state of paradise, the human race left behind its childhood and entered adolescence.

The Greek myth of Persephone is strikingly similar to the Hebrew one of Eve. Only here the seducer does not come as a snake, but in his own shape as Eros, god of desire. Persephone is not asked to pick a fruit, but a flower. When she has done this deed, showing that she has begun to live on her own in the present, she is immediately engulfed by matter, and becomes a dweller in the kingdom of dead stones. Persephone, too, eats a

---

1. Genesis, 3.5.

fruit, but later, at the request of Hades, not of Eros. In the netherworld she eats a pomegranate, symbol of marriage, to confirm her union with the regent of matter.

Of profound interest are the different ways in which these two sets of images depict the consequences of the rebellious deed. The Hebrew story makes the breach definite, but points toward hope for a faraway redemption. In the Greek story, the human soul is allowed to come back to paradise for half of her life, alternating with her stay in the world of matter. For the Greeks, heaven and earth were very close to each other.

Dionysus the Redeemer

The god Dionysus was also a child of Zeus and Demeter. As in the myth of his sister, Persephone, some of the deeds and sufferings of this god can be seen as depicting processes of vegetation and agriculture. Typical of Demeter's agricultural activities was growing grain for bread.[2]

When Dionysus was grown, he assisted his divine mother in her work and traveled everywhere throughout Greece and Asia Minor as far as India. Along the way he taught all the peoples he met the arts of cultivating plants and trees; more specifically the art of growing and pruning grapevines and of making wine from grape juice. In turn, he learned many things from his hosts and brought their oriental ideas and skills back to Greece. During his travels he was accompanied by a large retinue of bacchants and satyrs, humans and humanoids, who were attracted to him and were more strongly connected with nature than were average women and men. Demeter and Dionysus are the gods responsible for bread and wine, the two substances that represent all food and drink and, thereby, all earthly substances which human beings are able to tolerate within their bodies.

But just as in the myth of Persephone, there is much more to the story of Dionysus than a mere nature myth. The primary images in the Persephone story tell of her adolescence, and depict man's fall into the sphere of matter. The most remarkable images in the Dionysus myth are those that reveal what happened at his birth.

---

2. The Roman Demeter was called Ceres, whence the word cereal.

34

When Demeter gave birth to her son, the goddess Hera, the queen of the heavens, launched an attack on him that led to his destruction. Hera's spiritual being is the stately, but never yielding power of conservation. She preserves the established culture and defends it against all alien influences. She is strongly opposed to developments in men's ideas that could lead them in new, unproven directions. In mythopoetic language: She is extremely hostile to all illegitimate children of Zeus, and to their mothers, and tries to destroy or hinder them.

However, since Dionysus is the son of Demeter, a goddess like herself, Hera does not attack the mother, but the child. She summons to her aid the most conservative forces in the world, the dormant hierarchy of the Titans, the former generation of gods. They return from the past and, to please the mighty queen of heaven, take hold of the newborn Dionysus and dismember him. Because of this the son of Demeter is called *Dionysus Zagreus;* the surname, a Phrygian word, means "torn to pieces."[3]

Through the victory of the Hera forces, the arrival of the wine culture with all its consequences for the development of man's consciousness, was postponed. However, a child of god, a new spiritual idea, can never be destroyed. And so, a young virgin goddess, Athena, was invisibly present at the murder of the child. Athena found the heart of the little god child, his immortal being, still alive and gave it to his father, Zeus, who swallowed the heart and it became part of his own divine heart.

At a later time, Zeus fell deeply in love with a mortal woman, the Theban princess, Semele, whom he visited in disguise, and impregnated with the being of Dionysus. Hera was greatly upset when she learned what had happened, for she knew that this divine being, if allowed to be born, would eventually bring an end to the worship of the Olympian gods on earth. She considered it her duty to have the infant destroyed again. However, the second time, which occurred much later in the development of the world, she used more subtle means. She manipulated the feelings of Semele, so that she longed for her divine lover, and wished that once she might be allowed to see him as he really was.

---

3. Dionysus Zagreus was the main god in the rituals of an Eastern religion, called Orphism, after the mythical singer Orpheus. Orphism was particularly influential among the Ionian philosophers, Pythagoras most of all.

Through a cunning scheme, the princess got what she wished. She made Zeus confess that he loved her most of all; then she had him swear that he would grant her every wish. Since this oath was sworn "by the Styx," the river boundary of Hades, it was irrevocable even by a god. When finally she was sure of her position, Semele asked Zeus to prove his love by visiting her in his divine form. Zeus tried his utmost to dissuade her, but Hera gave Semele added strength, and she did not falter in her demand. Hera's expectation was realized, and for a short moment, Zeus confronted her as a god. Semele, unable to endure this direct contact with a divine being, caught fire. Spiritual fires began to consume her body, with the child unborn in her womb. But again Athena was present. She rescued the unborn child from his mother's dying body and gave it to Zeus, who hid it within his thigh. When the child was fully developed, he again came into the world out of his father's body.

It was in this second incarnation that Dionysus, now called *Dionysus Iakchos*, served as a helper to his first mother, Demeter, and taught people the use of wine. More than a natural beverage, wine has been spiritualized by the power of Dionysus. The fermentation process gives special qualities to the juice, which has effects that go beyond quenching the thirst of the body. This "blood of Dionysus" entered the blood stream of those who drank wine, enabling them to experience themselves in a new confrontation with their own awakened and enthusiastic individuality. This awakening led them to lose their dreamlike clairvoyance. It also led them to associate in wine drinking rituals with everyone, stranger or tribesman, who happened to be present, and this freed them from the exclusive bonds of the family.

When Dionysus sets out from the holy city of Delphi, his winter residence in the heart of Greece, he acts as one who teaches mankind how to enter a new state of consciousness, for which wine culture was a vehicle. Of all Greek gods, he is the only one who cares for men. The fact that, when he was born a second time, his mother was a mortal woman, made him akin to man. His dismemberment after his first birth by the powers out of the tribal past is an image that characterized Dionysus' activity in his next life, where he dismembers tribal attachments.

That Dionysus initially was prohibited from growing up as the son of Demeter caused the birth of man's individuality to be postponed. When he was reborn, it was on earth at a time when people were nearing the end of tribal pictorial thinking. Soon the "twilight of the gods" would be upon them.

The reality of reincarnation, which would later play an important role in the teachings of Orpheus and Pythagoras, is clearly shown in the myth of Dionysus. His first incarnation is very short and does not take place in the physical world; in his second incarnation he lives a full life on earth. During the time between his earthly lives, Dionysus lives absorbed within the being of Zeus. The depiction of Dionysus' reincarnation illustrates that when the ties with fathers and mothers, with family and tribe, are severed, man begins finding his center in his individual spiritual self. He now discovers that he has been his own ancestor, that he has inherited his present state of development from preceding stages of himself in former incarnations.

On his return from his travels Dionysus married Ariadne, "the very pure one," on the island of Naxos. He came to dwell in the temple at Delphi, which he shared with Apollo, the Olympian. Apollo, the radiant tribal god of the Greeks, who dwells in the light of the sun, is worshiped together with Dionysus, the divine spark of individuality, the spiritual being who dwells in each person. Macrocosmos and microcosmos are presented here as living under one roof. The Eleusinian initiates knew that Apollo and Dionysus were actually the same being. Dionysus also plays an important role in the temple school of Eleusis. In the crypt under the temple a mystery play was performed each September for a group of well-prepared pupils. In this play, Dionysus, the human self, redeemed his sister Persephone, the human soul, from Hades, the imprisonment of the physical world.

When the Olympian gods in nature were no longer accessible to people, they concentrated on Dionysus, the god within. When the temples were no longer maintained and the mysteries became decadent, the celebration of Dionysus migrated to the great and small theaters, especially the one in Athens. Here the priest of Dionysus had the seat of honor and here, on stage, the great riddles of life were presented for all to share. The holy mystery plays of Eleusis had evolved into "psychodramas" in which the whole audience participated with all the strength of their emotions.

In the Dionysus myth, the "fall" of man's soul into the sphere of the material world is depicted in its positive aspects as a developmental change of consciousness, moving from dreamlike

37

open clairvoyance in a state of "paradise," through dramatic pictorial thinking as members of the tribe, and then, during the last phase of the Greek culture, to consciousness of self as an individual spiritual being. The Greek ideal of morality, as expressed by Socrates, was to do good, on the basis of personal insight into what the circumstances demanded. In the Apollo-Dionysus temple in Delphi, one could read the admonition, "Know Thyself."

———

These are the most important Greek myths dealing directly with gods. In the Christian Heaven we find next to God and his angels legions of saints, represented in the stories of their lives as virtuous heroes. In the same manner, Greek mythology tells of many heroes, most of them demigods, who, through the performance of many good and heroic deeds, gain access to the spiritual world. They experience a sanctification, or rather an initiation, whereby these heroes introduce a new stage of culture to their people. They function as founders of cities, as representatives of new religions, as priests, and as kings.

THE ADVENTURES OF PERSEUS

Kings and other personages of myths and fairy tales did not live in a particular place or historical time; they are eternal beings who belong to us all, for they inhabit our inner lives.

Our earliest heroic myth begins with an episode from the life of an old king, whose name indicates no particular king, but a description.

Once there lived in Argos[1] a king, Acrisius by name, meaning "he who cannot make a choice." He was famous because of the great beauty of his daughter Danaë, that is "the Danaan woman." She was the most beautiful woman in the land, and Acrisius loved her dearly. He was proud and somewhat amazed that a child of his loins could have grown to such beauty. Sometimes, though, and gradually more often, he found himself wishing he had had a son instead, someone in whom he could find himself again in a fresh and unspoiled beginning. Anxious to know whether the divine world would still grant him this son, he traveled to Delphi to ask Apollo what fate had in store for him. The sacred moans and grumblings of the Pythia in trance made a strong impression on him, and when the attending priest began interpreting her utterances the king knew that the answer would be harsh. No longer would he be able to beget a son, the priest stated, but he would have a grandson. However, this son of Danaë would one day kill his grandfather in order to take his place. Bewildered and hurt, the old king went home and decided that he would try to circumvent fate, and had Danaë imprisoned in a tower of bronze, windowless, and built mostly underground. The only opening was in the roof to let some light and air enter. In this way Acrisius intended to make sure that Danaë could not become pregnant and give birth to a dreaded grandson who would become king in his place.

Listening to this narration, the ancient Greek audience knew that the king was wrong and sinful in his attempt to deceive the

---

1. Argos, land of the Danai, was a country in southern Greece, situated near the ancient city of Mycenae, the center of Mycenaean culture.

39

divine world and they began wondering how and when the unavoidable fulfillment of Delphi's prophecy would come about. Or, if they already knew the story, which almost always was the case, they could feel the structure of the myth beginning to shine through the tale. Underlying their appreciation of the singer's art was a patient attentiveness with which they awaited the realization of the prophecy at the end of the story. The narrator, on the other hand, would know the myth in all its details. It lives in his memory; he tells it "by heart," as if playing a concert instrument. He cannot read, and would have no use for notes. Reading and writing had not yet been invented in these "prehistoric" times of myth-producing thinking. The people who invented myths, or passed them on to others, did not consciously try to be artists. Art was an all-pervading quality of their culture. In everyday life they thought in living pictures dramatically interconnected with each other. Abstractions indicative of states of being or developments in time did not occur to their thinking. Their thoughts took a concrete pictorial form; instead of thinking "greed," they "saw" wolf. To understand such picture thinking we must translate it into abstract, logical thinking that we commonly use today. The interpretations in this book take as their point of departure the idea that all beings in Greek myths are depictions of man's inner tendencies and forces.

At the beginning of the Perseus myth, we meet Acrisius at the moment in his development when he has tuned his emotional life to such a fine harmony—indicated by his having a daughter of such great beauty—that the longing awakens in him for a strong, fresh impulse, a totally new beginning. Although the wish is born to have a son, his thinking is not clear enough for him to realize that his renewal cannot come from outside and that it should rather come forth as a metamorphosis of his developing feelings. When a new and higher form of his being is born, it will as a matter of course replace the self with which up to now he has been familiar.

Imprisoned in the tower, Danaë does not feel the loneliness, for she has substance and power enough within and memories sufficient to inspire her continued development. Light and air flow continuously to her from above. They convey the presence of the great god who lives in this illuminated air, father Zeus. He communicates with her by manifesting in the form of fine drops of gold that rain down upon Danaë, and soon she finds herself with child. In due time she gives birth to their son, a demigod, Perseus by name, meaning "the destroyer"—the destroyer of evil, as it becomes apparent in the course of the story. Although a not uncommon name, it is one that makes King Acrisius shudder. Apparently at this stage it was impossible for the king to halt his soul's development, try as he might, to deprive it of all sense perceptions and deny his emotions. His soul stays alive with its own forces of maturation, and the world of the gods remains accessible.

In frustration and despair the king wants his daughter and her child out of his sight. He has another prison made, this time a wooden chest not much larger than a coffin, in which they are cast upon the sea. For one entire night they sail in their dark confinement, bobbing up and down on the waves, the lovely Princess Danaë and her newborn child, warm in his *little red mantle*. The next morning they reach land and the chest comes to shore off the island Seriphus. There they wait for someone to rescue them and return them to solid land.

Now the king, afraid of the growing power of his young new being, gives up on the further development of his soul, and sends them over the waters to a different country—which means that he expects finally to have done away with them. From this point King Acrisius disappears into oblivion, returning at the end of the story to receive what we all know fate has in store for him.

The story of Acrisius and Danaë is the introduction to the myth of Perseus himself. He is a newborn semidivine being whose father is a god, and whose mother, Danaë, is the essence of the tribe of the Danai to which he belongs through her. The Mycenaean tribal name of Danaüs could also have been given to Perseus and it is important to note that Perseus was not fated to be a mere tribal being. Perseus is a hero, that is, an ideal human being whom all of us listeners should be happy and proud to look up to as our example in life. In the days of tribal culture, when this story was first conceived and told, many people must have felt a great desire to see before them the image of a real "individuality," someone able to develop his life on the basis of his own power without the support of mother or father, that is without the support of tribal customs or of ancestral traditions.

In mythopoetic thinking there exists a basic pictorial alphabet, in which the emblems father, mother, children are of great and specific importance. They can be translated or "understood" in the following way. My father ("my" because mythical persons are

41

within everyone of us) is concerned with the continuity and honor of our parentage. My father is my link with the past of the family, with my ancestors. My mother surrounds me with her warmth and her care; she protects and feeds me; she creates the mood and the style of family life. This home life is embedded within the cultural life of our tribe. My mother depicts the present. My children are my future. I bring them forth out of myself. They are my productions and my reproductions. My lovely, prudent daughter depicts what is developing within the life of my feelings, my emotional life. My willful, wild, courageous son depicts my inner willpower, the carrier of the essential activity that I call I, still young and growing. The ancient storytellers were in tune with the basic tendencies and stages of human growth, and could express through mythology their ideas of mankind's future development.

Like many other Greek heroes, Perseus is at birth abandoned by his family, in particular by his grandfather, with whom he will sever all connections after he has grown up and proven his mettle as an individual. In a stage of transition, carried by the waters of the night, the newborn hero sleeps enveloped in a little red mantle. No arbitrary embellishment, the mantle depicts the protective warmth of the hero's blood and accentuates the strength of this being in its growth toward individuality. Warmth is a very special "element"; one of the four elements we share with nature; we participate in air, water, and earth. The warmth within us, however, is our very own. We have to maintain its intensity throughout our lives, otherwise we become feverish and lose consciousness. The picture of the little red mantle represents the enveloping warmth of the blood, the vehicle of the forces of selfhood, which manifest themselves in the nuances of our consciousness. [2]

Although his mother accompanies him to the island and will feed and take care of him as long as he is dependent, her task on arrival is practically taken over by a foster mother, to whom she, being still young herself, becomes as a child. Perseus and Danaë are found by an old fisherman appropriately named Dictys, that is "net." A net is an instrument for catching what one needs without having to take the inessentials with it. The chest, floating in from the mainland, is the fisherman's catch of a lifetime. He and his wife

---

2. Little Red-Cap in Grimm's fairy tale of that name is a related image.

become the foster parents of both Danaë and Perseus, and at this point the hero starts the initial hidden stage of his development.[3] In modest circumstances he grows up completely on his own without traditions, either familial or tribal, to influence the manner of his life. Among the audience of the early storytellers there must have been young people who could enjoy this part of the myth as an ideal introduction to a secretly fancied life on one's own.

On approaching the independence of adulthood, which heroes, as a rule, experience earlier than we common people do, Perseus is confronted by Polydectes, the king of the island, who desires to marry Danaë. He happens also to be the brother of her foster father. Quite often a confrontation between two mythical beings depicts the meeting of a person with his reflection. In myth a being can see approaching him what in reality streams out of himself as a vice, a virtue, or a tendency. The hero's own aggressive attitude, for instance, will appear to him in the form of a sudden, ferocious tiger glaring into his face. Our hero, himself a royal prince in disguise, sees certain tendencies in his own development mirrored in King Polydectes. At this crucial stage of his life, where he has to make the choice of becoming either Perseus or a Danaüs, he feels a strong urge to take the easier way and fall back upon the traditional habits of the tribe, the urge to totally merge and identify with the tribe as the kingly husband of a Danaë. Instead of Dictys, "the catcher of the essential," now Polydectes, "the grabber of much," becomes to him the example of adult life. The danger confronting him is his own greed in the form of Polydectes. Unconsciously, his greed has already come to the decision to return to tribal life and become one of the Danai.

Greed, his reflected pseudoego, is already busy organizing a prenuptial feast to which not only all its friends, a group of vices, are invited, but also young Perseus, who is not aware that it is his mother whom the king intends to marry. All Polydectes' friends have a present for the bride-to-be; all but Perseus, the youngest of the guests. He is innocent of what is customary to greed and his fellow vices. He stands in their midst empty-handed and greatly ashamed. In youthful eagerness, he hastily promises to bring the king whatever he should wish. What is it that greed wants most? To have everything, of course; to have the ruling power of the world, to have the head, the essence, of Medusa. On hearing the dreaded

---

3. An episode common in the life of all young heroes.

name of Medusa, that is, "she who rules," the audience holds its breath and the storyteller makes a dramatic pause, for Medusa is the source of petrifaction which destroys life and soul.

People still of a mythopoetic frame of mind live in a strong, uninterrupted connection with living nature, which streams through them from all sides. This participation overwhelms their consciousness and makes it impossible for them to gain the distance needed for objective perception and reflection. They are, of course, not unaware of the mineral tendencies, the Medusa element, as an essential skeleton within the world and within themselves, but they easily avoid this factor in their thinking. It is not yet time for them to be put out of their paradisiac state into the hard, cold world of matter. Medusa rules the world by her deadening power of petrifaction and the enormous fear it inspires. Polydectes wants to have the power to make everyone, out of fear, give him whatever he wants. Then he would be able to paralyze his opponents. Greedy as his nature is, he takes it for granted that somebody should give him this power, namely young Perseus. Our real self, Perseus, has been tricked by our lower egoistic self, Polydectes, into either capturing the essence of matter, or perishing in the process. If we should acquire the coveted Medusa power, the Polydectes in us would be in possession of the ultimate Midas touch. Then, instead of participating in a living world, we would, through our materialistic attitude, turn nature into a storage room full of dead objects.

In the two introductory episodes of the myth, we have learned of Perseus' birth and of his growing up on the island. Now the storyteller is going to treat us to the myth of the grand, impossible mission that the hero will have to accomplish. This will gradually lead to the hero's initiation into nontribal, individual life, something which, for members of his audience, was still far in the future.

In a great hurry, without taking leave of his mother or his foster parents, Perseus sets out for Delphi. He seeks the oracle to tell him where on earth he can find the source of matter's great and dangerous power. However, the seeress at Delphi does not know the answer. The oracle, a typical tribal institution, cannot offer help for the problems of an individual's consciousness. The only aspect of his quest that the attending priest recognizes is its fundamental nature. The priest knows that the young visitor will have to go to the realm of the archetypes, which can only be approached through the world of the past. Therefore, Apollo sends Perseus to his father's oracle in Dodona. Here, the same thing happens; this oracle of Zeus cannot help him either. The Doves, as the priestesses are called at this sacred place, can only give him the assurance that the gods have their eyes on him. Then, while walking about in Dodona in great, silent expectation, Perseus becomes aware of a divine presence. Soon the wonderful moment arrives when Zeus' son and messenger, Hermes, the agile god of action, steps out of his invisible realm, the spiritual world, and becomes his friend and mentor. Immediately, Hermes points out to him that it would not be enough to be shown the place of the Gorgons, the name given Medusa and her two immortal sisters. To accomplish his impossible task he should also be properly equipped. Hermes, whose daily task it is to take the souls of the dead on their last great journey, now becomes Perseus' divine guide to the end of the physical world, that is, to the shore of Ocean, that wide river streaming around the edge of the terrestrial disc. Then he leads him to the other side, to the dusky intermediate area he knows so well from crossing it daily on his way to the spirit world. This is where the sisters of the Gorgons, the Graeae, live. As counterparts of the material forces within the realm of spirit, they will be able to help him on his way. These three sisters together form one threefold being, with one cyclopic eye and one tooth for the three of them to share. They are old gray birds, these Graeae, swans perhaps. But they have human heads, in which they place by turns their common eye and tooth.

Birds and bats in the dark form a common image in Greek pictorial thinking about the world of the dead. However, in confronting them, Perseus sees reflected the great guardian of his inner threshold. It is the same three-bodied being that Hercules encounters in Geryon, and the same being as the winged Sphinx that appears before Oedipus at one of the seven gates of Thebes. It is the image of his own threefold soul, its processes of thinking, feeling, and acting in a form not yet harmonized and unified. Its riddle has to be solved, that is, it has to be organized into harmony before entrance into the world of the spirit can be found. In the case of Oedipus, the solution is most explicitly given. The solution is MAN, the harmonized human being, presented in the three stages of his life. In Perseus' story the riddle is solved in an aggressive and playful way.

At the instigation of Hermes, Perseus captures the element that unites the three incomplete Graeae, that is, their solitary eye, and forces them to give the required information in exchange for its return.

The three Graeae, as if out of one mouth, tell him how to go to the land of the Hyperboreans, i.e., "the land beyond the north wind," where he will be equipped for his expedition. This fabulous land is not in the physical world and no physical ways lead to it. After passing the threshold guarded by the Graeae, the hero has to enter spirit land. Already before his death he is able to penetrate into the spiritual world under the guidance of Hermes, the initiator.

The "land beyond the north wind" looks like a picture of the paradise dream, mankind's golden age, a primordial state of lightness and innocence, a place full of festivities, music and dance, a good life in the midst of nymphs and angels. The guardians have shown Perseus the way back into the past of the human race, where the eternal gods, who do not live within space and time, enjoy an occasional visit. Apollo especially, and also his twin sister, Artemis, come to Hyperborea every winter. Perseus, introduced by Hermes, is received by the nymphs with friendly grace. He takes part in all the festivities and makes many friends. This is one of the most delightful mythical episodes, guaranteed to cheer the hearts of any audience. In later days, when myths no longer were alive, stories of eternal Hyperborea were still very popular, especially in books for children. For instance, we know from Plutarch's The Art of Teaching Poetry about a fantastic story, "Abaris," by Heraclides, that dealt with a Hyperborean of that name who managed to travel all over the world by holding on precariously to one of Apollo's shining arrows, as it was shot from the god's silver bow. During the first part of his initiation young Perseus experiences these archetypal inner developments as a spiritual being among others in the land of the spirit, and emerges equipped as a conscious spiritual individuality on earth. The nymphs have given him winged sandals, modeled after those of Hermes, so that he can fly and overcome physical gravity. They gave him a cap to wear, the cap of Hades, which makes him invisible to physical eyes, and also a purse, which can encompass anything by adapting its form and size, so that it is able to carry things that are not even in space.

On leaving this paradisal training ground, trying his wings, and eager to start his mission, Perseus realizes that he is not yet completely equipped and prepared. He still does not know where to look for the Gorgons, and hopes for Hermes' help in finding the right way. He will also need weapons, and wonders whether he will be worthy to receive such implements as only the gods can provide. He drifts away invisibly. But he does not have to wait very long. There again is Hermes' presence approaching from the right. Into Perseus' hand he puts the never-touched hilt of an adamantine sickle, made in heaven. Since Hermes hardly ever uses a weapon himself, we can assume that this is not his own, but one that the fire god, Hephaestus, has made especially for this important occasion. Now Perseus has the rank of a warrior, a knight with a sacred sword. But where will he find a shield with which to protect himself against the powers of petrifaction? There approaches from the left another divinity, the virgin goddess, Athena. She is full of assurance, calm, and wise. *Born directly out of Zeus' head she is the instrument of the gods' thinking, the brains of Zeus, appearing as an independent being. Since man is not able to endure direct contact with the awesome power of reality—it would either petrify him, or burn him up, as happened to Semele—nature in her wisdom equipped him with a cerebral reflector of great complexity. Brain thinking reduces the essential being of reality to a flow of images. That we can endure.* Athena, the ruler and patron of man's cerebral activity, now comes close to Perseus, who is soaring invisibly with Hermes at his right. On his left arm she places her own bright shield polished to mirror brightness. Looking at this as into a mirror, he will be able to come close enough to the power of matter to destroy it, without himself becoming petrified, that is, totally materialized.

And now the three beings soar forward over Ocean's boundary. The Gorgons do not live in heaven or in paradise, but, of course, on the physical earth itself. The gods guide the hero in the right direction. Perseus, now completely equipped, hovers high over the rocky island where the three sisters are sleeping. Medusa, being mortal and vulnerable, lies between her immortal sisters. While the divinities look on from above, the human hero descends invisibly and fulfills his incredible task. He severs the head of Medusa with one stroke of his divine sickle, while guiding his hand in accordance with the picture that comes up before his eyes in Athena's mirrorlike shield. When the head is off, Perseus puts it away in the fitting purse the Hyperboreans gave him. At the same time Medusa, through her severed neck, gives birth to the winged horse Pegasus which had been sired by the god Poseidon. Athena and Hermes now fade away into the sky. Perseus has done his work on his own; now he must take care of himself. He flies away as fast as he can. Medusa's sisters wake up. They see what has happened, jump into the air and pursue him with all speed. But he is safe in his invisible state and they cannot find him anywhere in the sky.

Thus Perseus overcomes the power of matter, the ruling queen of the world. Without her great and tragic head, Medusa looks like a winged dragon. Her naked body is covered with scales. Her wings of horn are formed like those of a bat. Her head is surrounded by hair made of thin snakes, capable of staring anybody down with the intensity of their glaring, lidless eyes. *She is the essence of physicality, the crushing condensation of weight, and the massive lifeless solidity of stone. When a man falls in love with her—which happens all the time—he becomes a compulsive materialist, an ardent collector of petrifacts. Polydectes, for whom Perseus had to capture Medusa's head, is just such an accumulator. His name, both in this form and in the variant Polydegmon, is often used as a characteristic of Hades, who in due time will "collect us all." By killing this force with the help of the divine weapons, and after a long training under soul-guiding Hermes, Perseus becomes a savior of man's evolution. He removes the forces of petrifaction that destroy life and soul. Had they gone unchecked, these forces would have turned the earth into an arena for robots. Perseus gives man the opportunity to stay productive in the life of his soul.*

The three Gorgons are the earthly sisters of the Graeae who guard the threshold "on the other side." In Medusa and her two immortal sisters we meet the fierce guardians of another threshold destined to scare man away as long as possible from the hidden realms of material existence, which in our time have proved to be deadly. Just as their sisters are comparable to the Sphinx, so the Gorgons have characteristics in common with threefold Cerberus, the terrifying hound of Hades. He too has hissing snakes for hair. As matter opens up and softens, Pegasus can be born among us out of Medusa's vocal chords. He is the winged horse who takes the poets on his back and flies with them to the wellspring of inspiration. He gives their songs life and wings.

Now Perseus goes on his way back home to bring Polydectes his due. He flies a roundabout way, as if he wants to survey the boundaries of the physical world, Medusa's former domain. Invisible, he glides over the southern land where the Ethiopians live, whom the gods often visit because they like them nearly as much as the Hyberboreans in the Far North. And it so happens that

he has to perform his Medusa killing again, this time all alone. Chained to a rock on the African shore, he sees a wonderful maiden. Already close by her in a cloud of foam, a water dragon, scaly and loathsome like an enormous alligator, rushes toward her. Perseus takes off his cap of Hades, at the same time descending at great speed. His hair stands on end and his eyes blaze. The maiden looks on unbelievingly how he kills the dragon with the sharp power of his divine sickle and sets her free. She is a princess, called Andromeda (i.e., "she who cares for man."). *Then, in confrontation, he recognizes in her his real self, the spiritual reality of his own being, the real goal of his dangerous quest. Having overcome the materialistic tendencies in himself, that is, having killed the greedy dragon that threatened to swallow his spiritual being, Andromeda, the eyes of his soul are opened. With her parents' grateful consent, they marry. Perseus unites himself with his spiritual form, who under the name of Andromeda is going to lead him through their joined life. Had he forsaken his quest for individuality, Medusa would have ruled him, as she did the tribal King Polydectes.*

There is another point of view from which one can understand the familiar image of a maiden chained to a rock. The image also depicts the human soul chained to the physical body. The Medusa force of Poseidon's sea dragon would have swallowed his soul completely and made her all stone, if Perseus had not appeared and destroyed the monster.[4]

There is yet a third point of view. The prophetic projection inherent in all mythopoetic images, timeless as they are, gives the Perseus development its historic place in circumstances where people are in the process of losing their religious foundations and are not yet able to find within themselves the means to organize their soul life. This shows up clearly in the background of the Andromeda episode. Her mother, Cassiopeia, queen of the Ethiopian people, i.e., the maternal power, the cultural life of that tribe, has in defiance boasted that she and her daughter are more beautiful than the daughters of the god of the sea. When a tribe no longer recognizes the superiority of the gods, they become remote and dim and eventually disappear altogether into a "Götter-dämmerung," a "dimming of the gods." Then, instead of populating their spiritual waters with gods, they find scaly monsters and

---

4. The well-known image of the archangel Michael as the dragon killer comes out of a similar inspiration.

their thinking becomes intellectual and infected with materialism. One of these monsters, a snakelike being, devours numbers of Ethiopians, until the queen decides to do what the oracle instructed and sacrifice her own daughter in expiation. If this sacrifice had been performed, the tribe would have lost its cultural identity, since the princess, as her child, is the essence of her mother, i.e., the tribal culture. Only Perseus, who is no longer living in mere tribal consciousness but who has developed himself into a true individual, is able to overcome the beast of materialism and rescue the soul of the tribe.[5]

United with Andromeda, Perseus then hastens home to the island of Seriphus. He finds his mother and his foster father in hiding from Polydectes, who cannot accept Danaë's refusal to marry him. Perseus meets Polydectes and his companions at a banquet and turns them to stone by presenting the Medusa head, which Polydectes had wanted so badly.

The king's greedy Midas wish thus turns upon himself. This death was foreseeable. The greed that Perseus felt rising in himself, and which he saw reflected in the person of Polydectes, was already destroyed in him when he killed the dragon before it devoured his newly found spiritual being, Andromeda. The variant reading of the myth, in which the dragon is not killed with the divine sickle, but petrified with the Medusa head, also makes sense as a prediction of what will happen to Polydectes. The rescue of Andromeda, the essence of Ethiopian tribal culture, from the devouring dragon finds a structural echo in the rescue of Danaë, the essence of the Mycenaean tribal culture, from her marriage to Polydectes.

The myth now enters its finale. Perseus makes his foster father, Dictys, whose modest net takes what should be taken, king in place of Polydectes, his brother. Perseus travels with both Danaë and Andromeda to Argos, where they want to pay a visit to his grandfather. But the old king flees as fast as he can, when he hears of the arrival of Danaë's son, and nobody knows where he went. Perseus, therefore, becomes king in his own right. But before he can settle down, he must first travel the world over. One of his journeys leads to the land of the Cyclopes, from where he brings back to Argos a number of brutish giants, each having only one solitary, circling eye. They build for him, out of gigantic blocks, the

---

5. Grimm's fairy tale "Little Red-Cap" has many similar motifs.

mortarless "cyclopic" walls of his new capital, Mycenae. This is the second time that we see Perseus in contact with one-eyed beings, representatives and stragglers of prehistoric cultures, whom he knows how to press into servitude. For the Perseus myth also tells the story of how the Mycenaean culture was founded by immigrating tribes who subdued the original populations. *In myths and in fairy tales, however, giants depict our instincts. They are dumb but strong and have to be kept in check; otherwise they grow too powerful for us.*[6]

Later, during another of his travels, King Perseus visits the king of Thessaly in his capital Larissa. As the king's guest, he is present at the funeral games in honor of the king's father who has just died. Being young and heroic, Perseus wants to participate in some contest. He chooses to hurl the disc. Again, to show his power over matter, he sends the heavy stone disc spinning through the air in a well-contrived trajectory. It goes on and on, much farther than any of his competitors'. But then fate steps in. Suddenly, the spectators perceive how the disc swerves off course and glides in their direction. They are all looking at it, their faces frozen with fear. The stone glides down, hits an old man and kills him: it is the old King Acrisius, who had been sitting there in disguise, and who, when he saw the fatal disc approaching, suddenly knew who had thrown it.

This accident fulfills the oracle, and brings the composition of the myth into balance.

Perseus has reached maturity. His mastery of the forces of matter brings a definite end to his connections with the past. The stone kills his ancestor. Now we see him before us as a hero, a human being who can actively support and develop himself with his own strength, and out of his own inner resources. His mother Danaë had been able to do the same, and this had led to his birth as a demigod. His grandfather, Acrisius, had a strong desire to gain this status of new independence, but shrank from the ultimate consequence.

In antiquity, the only way to acquire the spiritual independence of a true individual was to go through an initiation, to submit to the long training in a mystery temple, which, through exercises and trials, led to establishing contacts with the spirit world and

---

6. The Edda, the famous medieval book of Icelandic myths, presents us with giants of two different kinds and shows what will happen when they are left free.

finding before death one's orientation in the realm of the archetypes. (Plato calls them ideas, or forms.) The status of an initiate, however, is not a mere acquisition, but must be defended against temptations, and recaptured many times. Father Zeus approved of it, Dionysus gave the inner impulse, and both Hermes and Athena, supplying agile willpower and pure thinking, were always ready to help.

OEDIPUS

King Laius of Thebes, Boeotia's royal city, once traveled to Delphi
with courtiers and bodyguard to ask the oracle whether there was
any chance for him to become the father of a legitimate heir. The
absence of children in the palace had bothered him and his Queen
Jocasta. But hers was the greater grief, since the king had no lack of
"natural" children outside the walls of the palace. In the temple at
Delphi, which he visited in the evening, the Pythia went into her
trance for him. She stiffly held her white, contorted face up to the
light of the shining full moon. Her shrieks and moanings were wild
and foreboding. Although he had been there before, the king did
not feel at ease in this ill-smelling place. He expected the worst, and
therefore he was greatly surprised at the assurance of the attending
priest, whose task it was to interpret what Apollo spoke through his
mouthpiece, that he would indeed have a son by Jocasta.
However, before the unexpected happiness could begin to affect
him it was smothered and quickly turned to sorrow. For, after a
brief interruption, the priest went on: "This son of yours is destined
to kill his father, and then to marry his mother." Stricken and
speechless the king turned away. He left the temple not daring to
think. He mounted his traveling carriage, and was driven home,
brooding and silent. Arriving at his palace, he told Jocasta what
answer Apollo had given, and the thoughts he eventually had
formed on the way back from Delphi. As a solution, he suggested
they should no longer live together as husband and wife, so that
this child of doom would not be allowed a chance to come into the
world.

*But, as we all know, to deceive the gods is simply not possible.
They live beyond time, beyond past, beyond present and future.
They survey the world and the patterns of its development from an
Olympian point of view.*

Once, after a feast during which the drinking of too many cups
of wine had undermined the king's strength of character, never
very great at any time, Jocasta and Laius again slept together. The
ensuing pregnancy, her first, was a terrifying experience for the

very young queen, since its outcome would inevitably bring the greatest of sorrows. When her son was born, they named him Jocastus, "the unique one," after his mother, as if to indicate that the king disclaimed all responsibility. The young mother was very soon compelled to surrender her dear child, whom the king gave to one of his shepherds. This faithful servant was to take it into the wilderness and there abandon it to its fate.

The role, which King Laius, the father of Jocastus-Oedipus, plays in this myth, is very similar to that of King Acrisius, Perseus' grandfather, though in character he is less refined and more forceful. After he has assigned the child to be left in the wilderness, he leaves the stage, just as Acrisius does, to come back only when his fate is to be fulfilled. In his own development, Laius is handicapped by his lack of courage. Although in Jocasta he has discovered his spiritual counterpart, his uniqueness as a spiritual being, he longs to go on seeking his spirituality in many insincere attempts to rejuvenate himself and in so doing he becomes the father of numerous bastard children. Nevertheless, his real development continues, and he is about to discover his true form renewed in his legitimate son. Then, like Acrisius, he shrinks from giving up the set of habits he has grown used to calling "I," and tries to forestall the birth of his new self.

Oedipus, whose story begins at this point, is from the beginning destined to become a hero. He starts life as an orphan in exile. Without benefit of ancestral or tribal guidance, he has to make a life of his own in his own way.

The shepherd plays a small but important part in this myth. As a trusted servant, he is the king's close companion, or rather, he is part of the king's soul, a positive element in his master's character. Every king can be seen as a shepherd, a leader of his people, who takes care of them as his own family. When Laius entrusts his rejuvenated newly born being to the hands of his shepherd, he does not really want it to be destroyed. He knows in his heart that his shepherd will take care of it, and that he will have to meet his son again, when the time will be ripe.

The threads of many fates cross when the Theban flocks, going south, mingle with the Corinthian sheep. Through his shepherd, each king reaches out to the other. The unwanted child is taken over by the royal couple of Corinth, who, childless, are delighted to become its foster parents. Here, but a four days' walk south from the town of his birth, young Oedipus grows up, well cared for and loved.

His young years are uneventful until he is nearly grown, when he starts to have doubts about his identity. He meets another young man, who is angry at him, and tells him bluntly that he is an adopted child. In this crisis—a confrontation with his impatient self in a mood of insecurity—Oedipus needs to know the truth. On his own initiative, without asking his foster parents the important question, or taking leave of them, he travels the coastal road from Corinth to Delphi. On seeing him in the sanctuary, the priest realizes that here is one who is fated to kill his father and marry his mother. He tells him so directly. Instead of hearing about his origin, Oedipus is told his destiny. He is shocked to the core of his being, and his insecurity is now unbearable. Now he is not only without known ancestors, but also without an imaginable future. He decides never to go home again, never to return to Corinth. Leaving Delphi, he takes the main road that leads due east to Thebes, and from there continues to the south, toward Eleusis and Athens.

Meanwhile in Thebes, King Laius, although aware of the sinful attempt of deception he had perpetrated twenty years ago, is in such a predicament that he ventures to visit Apollo's oracle again. Thebes, his city, is watched and besieged by a monstrous being. The Sphinx lies there in wait, and makes her nightmare presence felt at one of the seven gates of the city. Unless he can solve her riddle, no one can enter the town of Laius' tribe. Many citizens and many visitors, unable to answer her question, have been strangled and eaten by the monster. The king, with four servants, travels west towards Delphi, to learn from Apollo's oracle how to overcome this terror. As he travels, he comes closer and closer to the unexpected meeting with his son, who is walking eastward on the same road.

The audience listened to the performance of this well-known tale while seeing before their minds' eye the two royal men of different generations steadily approaching each other, heading for their fateful confrontation. Oedipus walks as if in a dream, choked with rage against his incomprehensible fate. His head bent, he pays no attention to people he encounters or to the land around him. When the sound of a horse and carriage, for some time vaguely sensed, comes too close to be any longer ignored, he stands still and looks up. The old man, who meanwhile has stood up from his seat, is forced to stop his horse. Both men look at each other in a malevolent tension. The king had never expected that he should have to stop. In his sharp commanding voice he orders the insolent young stranger to step aside and lifts his horse whip in warning. At the sight of this gesture Oedipus' fury explodes and all his rage streams out in one fierce and silent attack. He brings the old man down from his carriage and when he surrenders, swiftly kills him.

At the moment he felt his life endangered the king must have bitterly realized that this assailant was his long lost son, for Apollo's prophecy had never been far from his memory. Oedipus' rage was not yet spent and he slew three of the king's companions. The fourth man, a shepherd, escaped in the wilderness. All this happened at a crossroads. There would have been room enough for them to pass each other.

Prince Oedipus has been exiled from two tribal cultures, at birth from Thebes by his parents, at maturity from Corinth through his own volition. By unwittingly murdering his father he has severed all connections with his ancestors. He stands alone at the beginning of his life as an individual.

It must have taken him many days to arrive, on foot, in the neighborhood of Thebes, which towers on top of a hill. The city was still under siege and the situation in the town had deteriorated. The king, since he had not returned, was supposed dead. The leaders of the people decided to offer the king's power and position to anyone who could prove that he was able to lift the siege and restore the life of the tribe. When Oedipus arrived at the outskirts of Thebes, he sensed the mood of city and countryside, the fear and the gloomy silence. From a man who pointed to a huge rock by the side of the main gate, he heard about the Sphinx sitting there in the distance. She is a terrifying being, an uncanny outrage with a superb woman's face and shapely breasts, gigantic eagle wings, and shiny, gruesome claws, for she is also a lion. Curious people in town sometimes climb high upon the wall above the gate to peer down, and afterward tell about the graceful monster cat and the endless murders she perpetrates. Oedipus also hears about the reward offered to anyone who can overcome the Sphinx. He feels greatly attracted to this challenge. With his unthinkable prospects he has nothing to lose. His mood becomes light and foolhardy. He saunters up to the awesome presence. The Sphinx has been following him with her turning eyes, holding herself perfectly still. He is fascinated by her and, strangely, it is as if in some way he has known her all his life. For a moment she looks down at her claws and flexes them for inspection. Then, when he is close, she turns

the shine of her two great eyes fully upon him and in her cool and solemn voice demands that he solve her riddle: "What being, with only one voice, has sometimes two feet, sometimes three, sometimes four, and is weakest when it has the most?"

Oedipus studies her carefully, while thinking about his answer. He notices her lion's body, her eagle's wings, and human head, a threefold inhuman hybrid, an inhabitant of dreams. And the answer of her riddle rises up in him as an illumination: that being is MAN. When young he crawls on all fours; growing up he uses his two legs and feet; and in old age he needs a walking stick as a third leg. On hearing this, the Sphinx lifts herself up on her batting wings and soars high over the city, taking the nightmare of doom with her, and falls to her death. The road is free. Oedipus sees the heavy wings of the giant doors slowly turning on their pivots. He hears the joyful shouting inside streaming out to welcome the redeemer. Feeling himself completely free, he stretches, stands tall, and strides over the threshold into the town. This is his city from now on. On the same day he is declared king and married to the queen of Thebes. On this day his personal development is put to the side.

Oedipus who grew up in exile without any paternal influence, was pressed by fate and chance[1] to sever once and for all the last unconscious vestiges of this connection. He did not choose to take another direction at the place where his and his father's lives crossed. Instead he collided with the king and killed him. In his desperate loneliness he then approached the tribe. In this myth there are two different images of the tribe, one of the mother, the other of the city. Thebes, his city, is depicted as having seven gates, which characterizes it as being a heavenly, a cosmic city. Wherever the number seven occurs, the original storyteller had also the macrocosmos in mind with its seven gates, representing the seven planets. A city on earth was always built around a central well, forming a vertical connection with the spiritual world.[2] The earthly city was considered the manifestation of a spiritual city. The city as the dwelling place of tribal gods and men was experienced as a living being. The wall around it was its skin;

---

1. Our fate is to a great extent the consequence of our deeds in the past, while a new chance often befalls us unexpectedly in the course of our life.

2. That is where the good girl sits spinning the thread of her fate in Grimm's fairy tale "Mother Holle."

the gates, its connections with the outer world, the senses. The tribe in this myth appears to be at a crucial stage of its development. No inhabitant is allowed to enter without giving proof of knowledge of self as a human being. King Laius—his name is derived from laos, *meaning "people"—is bewildered by this emergence of individuality in his people, and seeks advice from Apollo. The Delphic oracle, a tribal institution itself, plays an important role in this myth.*

The being appearing as the Sphinx is the guardian at the threshold of man's self-knowledge. She is able to guard all seven gates, for, as a supersensible being, she is not bound to earthly situations—she is equipped with wings. She is also a composite being, consisting of eagle, lion, snake (tail), and man. Dominated by the animal in her, she is a picture of instinctive man. Everyone confronted by this being should see her as the mirror image of his own animality. Because Oedipus was the only one far enough developed to have this experience, he was the only one who could answer the riddle that she posed. The Greek writer Pausanias, a collector of travel anecdotes, mentions that the Sphinx sometimes was believed to have been an illegitimate child of Laius. As Oedipus' half sister she has much in common with him (with all of us), and therefore he can understand her riddle.

Having withstood the trial of self-knowledge, Oedipus is able by an act of his own free will to identify himself with the tribe of the Thebans, that is, to marry their queen.

Oedipus made an excellent king, one who considered all of his people his children. Four children of their own were born to Jocastos and Jocasta, two boys and two girls. For the Thebans they represented the rejuvenation of the tribe in the duality of the sexes and the quadripartition of the temperaments. With his own children Oedipus could be both happy and sad; with his people Sophocles describes him as experiencing the same feelings.

Overcoming the Sphinx, the guardian of Thebes' threshold, is a powerful experience of selfhood for Oedipus. Here he stepped over the threshold into the first stage of his initiation. A twofold renewal of his being is depicted in the births of his two sons, a new way of thinking and a new way of acting. This stage of inner development as a beginning initiate coincided with his life as king of the tribe, the first half of his life as an adult. When this stage reached its maturity, indicated by the fact that his elder son, Polynices, came of age, the time had come for Oedipus to take further steps in his own evolution. Now the power of tribal culture had to retreat in his life. Around him a massive dying away began of people, beasts, and plants; pestilence was followed by famine. The queen's brother, Creon, was sent to Delphi to learn the cause and the remedy. The indication of the oracle was clear: "Seek and punish the forgotten murderers of Laius!"

Oedipus again was compelled to move further towards his individualization. First he had to learn that in killing the old man he overcame his father, his ancestry, and that this made it possible for him to become aware of himself in confronting the Sphinx. and to install himself as king of Thebes. Yet it also obliged him to continue on the path he had begun.

The rest of the myth is told in many variants. The one used and dramatized by Sophocles is not archetypal, but very tragic. In rightful indignation at his people's and his own forgetfulness, Oedipus cursed the murderer of King Laius, for the sake of whose guilt his beloved city had to suffer so greatly. The first thing that came to his mind was to send for Tiresias, the blind, old[3] soothsayer of Thebes. Tiresias, however, was reluctant to come, for he had known all the time of the fateful tragedy that brought the great King Oedipus to the throne. Now he stood before him, leaning on someone's shoulder, his head bent, his face closed, without a word. When Oedipus became irritated at the old man's attitude, Tiresias warned him and all the others foolish enough to probe in what would better remain secret, saying that great suffering would come from knowing the truth in this matter.

The king did not give up. He asked everyone old enough to have heard of the circumstances of Laius' death, the old servant who had escaped the attacker and Queen Jocasta. Gradually, a bitter suspicion grew in him when he thought of the old man in his carriage, whom he had killed outside Delphi a few days before confronting the Sphinx. Unexpectedly, his spirits lifted when a messenger from Corinth arrived announcing the death of his king. To his great relief Oedipus felt that the oracle had been in error since it was clear that he had not killed his father. But the messenger, an old man, set the record straight, telling him that he was not the son of the Corinthian king, but had been adopted. The

---

3. The incredibly old Tiresias plays a role in many myths. The name means, "he who loves omens." It could as well be a word for "clairvoyant prophet."

messenger himself had taken him as a baby to Corinth. Saying so, he pointed toward a Theban servant who had been a shepherd like him and had given him the child. At this moment Queen Jocasta left the meeting, went to her room and hung herself. Oedipus continued asking questions and realized that the former shepherd was the same man who saved himself by running away when Oedipus murdered his own father. With the enormous tension of total silence, he stands up and leaves the room to look for Jocasta. When he finds her dead, hanging in her room, he takes the broaches from her dress and puts out his own eyes.

Oedipus shows that he is not able to take the next step on the path of self-development, which would have been to resign in favor of his son and begin a new phase of life outside his Theban tribe. Instead, he clings to the tribal setting which had given him so much joy and importance. His mother's having taking her own life signifies that the tribe had let him go. Oedipus, however, does not dare consider his situation in its true significance; instead, he blinds himself.

The second part of his mature life is but a weak repetition of the first. Oedipus, blind and powerless, is merely tolerated by the new ruler Creon, Jocasta's brother. Guided by his daughters, he wanders aimlessly through Thebes. The time comes when his sons begin to assert themselves. With Creon's consent, perhaps at his instigation, the old king is expelled by his people. Led by his older daughter, Antigone, a paragon of strength—in other words, led by his emotional life, now strong through suffering—Oedipus returns to the road on which he came to Thebes from Delphi many years ago. Slowly he walks on, and continues until he enters the city of Athens in Attica. There the young King Theseus receives him with great honor and friendship and gives him a place to live in a beautiful grove where he soon dies. After Oedipus' death many people liked to visit Colonus, where he lived at the end of his life. They paid their respects to the hero who solved the riddle of the Sphinx and thus saved his city, to the king who had been so good to his people, and to the man who had shown himself very human in not being able to complete his development, and who, finally, through great suffering, went the lonely road to the spiritual world.

———

N.B. The Oedipus myth, the most important in Greek culture—according to Aristotle—also figures prominently in the thinking of Siegmund Freud. However, the aspects Freud accentuates in his psychoanalytical theory are absent from the pictorial fabric of the myth. The psychoanalytic interpetation of the myth, valid as it may be for the guidance of a type of therapeutic thinking, is, from a mythopoetic point of view, a misuse, and does not interpret the myth in any essential way.

HERCULES, THE GREATEST OF ALL HEROES

After her wedding ceremony in the great city of Thebes, Princess Alcmene was accompanied to her bridegroom's house by a procession of relatives and friends, but not by her husband. He, Amphitryon of Tiryns, although a foreigner in exile, had become the greatly honored commander in chief of the Theban army. It so happened that just after his wedding a message was brought, indicating that he was needed at the border to organize a battle against intruders. Without a word to anyone, he left the wedding party. In the evening, when he felt sure that all was quiet, he again mounted his horse and took the shortest route back to the city, where he knew his beloved wife was waiting for him. Alcmene, meanwhile, was under the mistaken impression that he was already there. For Zeus, leader of the Olympian gods, had taken on the perfect likeness of the victorious bridegroom. So it came about that Princess Alcmene soon was expecting not one but two children, one fathered by Zeus, the other by her husband Amphitryon.

When the time had come for her to give birth to her twins, the women who were present to assist her were distressed to see that there was no progress. As with all births, not only were mortal women visiting in the room, but also invisible, divine beings. In the first place stood Eilithyia, the goddess of birth. She could not come close to help the young mother-to-be because of the majestic presence of her own divine mother, the goddess Hera. The queen of the heavens was sitting invisibly in front of Alcmene's bed, assuming the attitude of "looking in," all the while holding her ankles, legs, arms, wrists, and fingers crossed, and her lips and eyes tightly closed, so that no birth could possibly take place. In this atmosphere of mounting tension, one of the servant girls, who had knowledge about such things, became convinced that there was magic involved. Being a smart and slightly reckless character, she suddenly jumped up with a loud and enthusiastic outcry, as if to express her joy that at long last a child was coming into the world. Everyone present frowned at her behavior and muttered unfriendly sounds. Hera, startled by the unexpected noise, lost her concentration. When Hera relaxed her locked attitude, Eilithyia took a few steps forward and helped the princess give birth to twin sons, Hercules and Iphicles.

At the earliest moment of his life, we see Hercules pursued by Hera, the goddess after whom he was named. Her divine ill will for this son of her divine husband is one of the shaping forces of his life. Zeus loved this half-immortal son of his more than the many others he had fathered and had great expectations for him. Once, Zeus made a half serious, half defiant attempt to win his wife's sympathy for his little son. As Hera lay fast asleep, Zeus, faster than a thought, went down to earth and took the sleeping Hercules up with him to Olympus. He laid the baby at Hera's breast, but the infant Hercules, already showing some of his later wildness, bit the goddess painfully and she pushed him away in disgust. Some of the divine milk spilled from his lips over the night sky, forming the Milky Way, still there for all to see. Zeus hastened to bring him back home. Nursed as he had been by a goddess' milk, Hercules was now immortal.

When the twins were but one month old, Hera launched a vicious attack on little Hercules and sent two serpents to crush him in their coils. In the dark of the night, the two monstrosities slithered along the floor of the room where the infants were sleeping. When the snakes rose straight up on either side of his brother's crib, little Iphicles woke up and shrieked. But Hercules, who was developing much faster than a common child, sat up straight, took a snake in each hand, and proudly showed his parents, who came running with lights, that he had paid his attackers in kind. He had strangled them both.

Delaying the birth of one of her husband's illegitimate children was not an uncommon tactic of Hera's. When the Titaness Leto was about to give birth, she, too, was harassed by Hera. No place on earth dared let her stay long enough and in great anxiety she traveled in all directions, until at last she set foot on the floating island of Delos, which immediately anchored itself to the bottom of the Aegean Sea to give her the rest and support she needed. She now could bring the twin gods, Artemis and Apollo, both children of Zeus, into the world. Delos gained importance as the seat of an oracle of Apollo and for a great festival of music and gymnastics that took place each spring in honor of Apollo and Artemis. Another woman, who like Alcmene became the mother of twin children, one the son of Zeus, one of the royal father, was Leda, queen of Sparta, who was visited by Zeus in the form of a swan. Her children were the well-known heroes Castor, the mortal one, and Pollux, or Polydeuces. She also had two daughters, Helen (of Troy), the immortal daughter of Zeus, and Clytemnestra, the tragic wife of Agamemnon, king of Mycenae.

For Hercules, Hera's attempts to punish Zeus through his son and his paramour had tragic consequences. Alcmene was not the only granddaughter of Perseus, the founder of Mycenae, who was expecting a child. So, too, was Nicippe, the reigning queen of Mycenae. On the morning of the day destined for the birth of Hercules, Zeus boasted that before nightfall a son of his would be born who would rule over all men of his kin, that is, over all the offspring of Perseus. Hera made Zeus confirm this word with an oath, so that it could not be revoked. As a result of her magic interference at the side of Alcmene's bed, Eurystheus, the son of Queen Nicippe, was born first, and in due time became king of Mycenae. As a consequence, Hercules, whom Zeus apparently knew before his birth and had destined to be king, and thus his representative on earth, became a mere vassal of his cousin Eurystheus.

Zeus, the father of gods and men, is the divine creative power who constantly brings new elements (children) into the stream of the living world. Many such children of Zeus are born of the mortal women he loves. They grow up to be semi-divine heroes and the leaders of tribes. If these processes of creation should go unchecked, the whole course of history and the development of the different cultures would become unbalanced. The power of Zeus' wife, Hera, exists to prevent this. She is a stern and stately goddess who hates to see Zeus directly intervene in the social life of the Greek states. Hera's function is to preserve Greek culture. In the case of Hercules, she intended to keep the tribal rules of royal succession in force without any interruption from this unexpected, and probably unpredictable half god.

Like Achilles and other demigods, Hercules is often overwhelmed by the divine powers within him, which he cannot always master. In fits of diminished consciousness, he is prey to angry, mean behavior. In the many myths told about him throughout the Mediterranean, he shows a double image: sometimes appearing as the greatest of all heroes, nearly equal to the Olympian gods whom he often assists in battle against their enemies; at other times he is just a clumsy and brutish man, too strong for his own good. His depiction as the divine one of twins merely indicates his two-sided personality. An additional indication is the fact that the only role his twin, Iphicles, ever plays is as occasional helper to his brother, although his name means, "well known for his strength." In him we should see not so much a separate being, as the earthly component of the composite half god Hercules, whose real name means "well known because of Hera," that is, "because of his struggle with Hera."

It is characteristic of the majority of Greek heroes that they show their destiny to become independent by growing up without direct contact with their fathers. Usually the heroes are exiled. However, this did not happen to Hercules, the greatest of the Greek heroes. His battle against tribal influences and heredity took place on a much loftier plane. He had continually to overcome the direct influence of the goddess Hera herself, who wanted him to stay within the standard rules of tribal and familial traditions. This was the battle of his life, and it gained him the hero name Hercules.

After receiving a martial education from the greatest experts, Hercules spent many years of his youth as a cowherd in the mountain pastures. He enjoyed this hidden life in nature and matured quickly. He came into the open at the age of eighteen by killing a huge and dangerous lion, the terror of the mountain ranges near Thebes. This feat made the young herdsman well known as a courageous fighter of enormous strength. Shortly afterwards he performed a second great deed for the benefit of the Thebans. Showing himself a good son of General Amphitryon, he defeated, with soldiers, the king of neighboring Orchomenus and Thebes was no longer forced to pay tribute to this enemy. As a reward, the king accepted him as his son-in-law. Hercules was still very young, but he and his wife, the equally young Princess Megara, had a good life together, and before long they became parents of three children.

By defeating the aggressive lion (in his heart) Hercules developed the great virtue of courage. He was now considered an adult hunter and warrior, and at eighteen he had already renewed his threefold being in the three children he sired. This development, however, was premature. It had been accelerated as a consequence of the powerful divine forces in him. Young Hercules was overreaching himself, and the moment came when he was no longer able to sustain this level of consciousness. His life lost its structure and orientation. Now Hera saw her way clear to bring the hero back into the fold and undo his life as an individual. She made him destroy all he had developed in himself in one murderous deed. Under a cloud of madness he killed his three children and his wife. In a dramatically powerful way, the myth presents a strong warning, pointing to the dangers of premature development, which often ends in disaster, or, less tragically, simply evaporates. When Hercules realized what had happened, he felt desperate and wanted to kill himself too. This was the moment when Theseus, the young king of Athens, stepped out of the future to help the hero find himself again, just as he had done for Oedipus towards the end of his life. Theseus showed a total disregard for Hera and the common taboos of old; he represented a new force in life. He took the bewildered and depressed Hercules by the hand without any fear of the contagious pollution with which, according to tradition, a murderer is burdened. Theseus acted on his own out of human love when he took Hercules from Thebes to start a new life with him in Athens. Soon afterwards Hercules was able to take hold of himself again. He decided to go to Delphi to learn from the oracle what he should do to expiate his enormous sin.

Although his father, Zeus, did not give any help to his beloved son, Theseus, the archetypal human being, whose name means "he who organizes," could appear within Hercules. Such partial awakening of his true individuality was the result of suffering. It foreshadowed the ego force of his real being, which completely awakens within him at the end of his twelve labors. This "Theseus-phenomenon" put Hercules back on his feet. However, he was not yet able to live by himself in the atmosphere of self-reliance that typified the life of a true Athenian. He had to return to the tribal oracle of Delphi to learn what he should do.

The oracle, by sending Hercules to his cousin Eurystheus, the king of Mycenae, demanded of him the ultimate humility and patience. Hercules had to ask this man of no great account, who occupied the position Zeus had wanted to bestow on him, for adequate punishment. Eurystheus directed him to perform twelve nearly impossible tasks. *They would constitute his purgatory, and would take twelve years to fulfill. In this confrontation with the legitimate king of the Mycenaean people, he comes face-to-face with certain forces and tendencies in his own heredity that he must overcome completely now that he is intent on making a new beginning in a mature, unhurried way.*

To perform these labors, he first traveled through the northern part of the Peloponnesus on a circular route. Near the town of his mother's family, in Mycenae, he performed his first labor, or trial, near Nemea. Then he went a bit south to Lerna, then west, then north, finally back east through the land of Arcadia, the mountainous country of Artemis, finishing westward in Elis. After withstanding the first six trials close to home, the second half took him all over the Mediterranean world and beyond. After each mission, he had to return to King Eurystheus in Mycenae to show what he had done and to receive his new assignment.

These travels depict his inner journey on the path of self-development. At each of the twelve stations he is confronted by tendencies in himself that he has to capture, tame, and sometimes destroy.

In the first group of three trials, killing the lion of Nemea is the most important and characteristic deed; in the second group, it is killing and chasing away the Stymphalian birds; in the third, capturing the Cretan bull; and in the last group of three, the removal of Cerberus, the guardian dog of Hades, after which Hercules could enter the spirit world and so come to initiation. The images of lion, bird (i.e., eagle) and bull depict the three essential functions of man's soul: namely feeling, thinking, and willing or doing, respectively represented by the rhythmic, the nervous, and the metabolic systems of the body.

The Twelve Labors of Hercules

As his first labor, Hercules was sent out to the mountainous area north of Mycenae, where, in the neighborhood of the town of Nemea, a monstrous lion was causing great damage and fear. It was characteristic of this Nemean lion that it could not be wounded by any weapon; Hercules, therefore, had to catch and fight it bare-handed. When the hero discovered where the lion lived, he blocked off one of the den's two openings with large rocks; then he chased the animal inside. He approached the growling monster, wrestled with it, pressed it to his chest, lifted it off the ground, and finally squeezed it to death. Exhausted, the hero rested for a while and dressed his wounds. Then he set out to skin the lion, which

71

could be done only by using the monster's own claws as flaying knives. The head with its manes he left attached to the hide, removing only the lower jaw. After cleaning and tanning the skin, he wore it as a perfect body armor; the attached skull with its streaming manes he wore as a helmet. Hercules had become a lion man.

Some sources relate that the Nemean lion, a supersensible being, was an offspring of the primordial fire monster Typhon, the last-born child of Uranus and Gaea, and of Typhon's daughter, the serpent woman Echidna. It was also the brother of the Theban Sphinx, that heterogeneous composite of human, lion, and bird. Signs of the zodiac that reflect Hercules' deeds are Leo (Nemean lion, first labor), in a quadrature with Aquarius (Augeas, sixth labor), Aquila (i.e., Scorpio) (Stymphalian birds, fifth labor), and Taurus (Cretan bull, seventh labor).[1]

Hercules begins his new path by attempting to acquire the right idea of himself. He first has to overcome his innately boastful attitude, his lionesque front with its waving manes and frightening roar. To learn who he is, he has to establish an intense contact with this aspect of his being and deprive it of breathing power. What remained he turned into an impenetrable garment of defense, which he could then put on or take off in accordance with his own free will.

As his second task, Hercules was ordered to destroy the Hydra, a water snake living in the marshland of Lerna near Argos. The Hydra was the sister of the Nemean lion and of the Sphinx, a monster older than the Olympian gods. This supersensible being appeared as a dragon with nine heads. Cutting them off had a generative effect, as Hercules soon found out, because out of each neckwound there sprouted two new heads. In this labor Hercules was helped by his nephew Iolaus, the son of his brother Iphicles. Each time Hercules cut off a head, Iolaus stood ready to cauterize the stump with torches. While Hercules was engaged in battle with the Hydra, Hera sent an enormous crab to bite him in the heel. Hercules crushed the crab under his foot. Since then it has a place in the zodiac as the constellation Cancer.

When all the heads were off and the wounds could no longer sprout new ones, Hercules took the central head, which was immortal, and buried it under a pile of rocks. He then dipped his

---

1. See W. Sucher, *Isis-Sophia* (Broad Oak, Shropshire, Engl.: Willy Sucher, 1952).

arrows in the Hydra's poisonous blood. Never would the wounds they inflicted heal.

With its nine swaying heads and its tendency to grow forever, expanding by bifurcation, the Hydra resembles a monstrous tree—an image of the abundance of growing forces in Hercules. After having corrected his attitude in performing his first labor, Hercules' second step of preparation was to prune his overwhelming physicality and purify it by fire. He also put the source of his life's power, the immortal head, definitely within the stone house of his physical body.[2]

Now Hercules was equipped to perform the next two labors. First he must capture, not kill, a dangerous wild boar living in the mountains of Arcadia. Even though a boar is a fearless and savage animal, to kill it would not have been too difficult for a hero of the power of Hercules. Instead, he was obliged to capture it alive.

On his way to the mountains he had an additional adventure. For a day he stayed with a friend, the centaur Pholus, a hybrid of horse and man who gave him a good meal and opened a vessel of wine for him. This wine was not really the property of Pholus, but belonged to his kin. When the other centaurs smelled their wine being poured, they raced to the spot with a great clatter of hooves and a fierce battle broke out. To defend his friend and himself, Hercules was obliged to participate. He shot some of the centaurs with his poisonous arrows; others fled at the sight. Unfortunately, he also hit Chiron, the wisest of all centaurs, the famous teacher of heroes. Chiron suffered greatly from his incurable wound, so much so that later he was willing to sacrifice his miserable life to help Prometheus become free.

Continuing his journey into the mountains, Hercules soon discovered the boar. He frightened the animal and it ran away. Then he laid down his weapons and gave chase. But the boar was much too fast for him. Finally, he thought of a method to immobilize the animal. He drove it into a deep snowbank. Capturing it there, he carried it on his enormous shoulders to King Eurystheus, who shivered at the sight of the fierce monster and hid in a large storage urn.

Hercules took the animal back to the Erymanthian mountains and set it free. Then he hastened to Thessaly where he joined the

---

2. Houses, stables, and sometimes vehicles are mythopoetic images of man's physical body.

Argonauts in their quest for the Golden Fleece.

In his third labor, Hercules learns to control the fierce aggress-iveness that sometimes could drive him to murder. By means of relentless training he gains the insight through which he could uproot this tendency. In the cold purity of "snow white" thinking,[3] he is enabled to deprive the aggressive instincts of their footing. Hercules often met centaurs, images of instinctive man, and felt at home with them. While visiting with centaurs he immersed himself in his own instincts. Not yet strong enough to keep his instincts well in hand, he must go through great turmoil, in the course of which the wisest of all his instincts is wounded. Eventually, Hercules will have to sacrifice instinctive wisdom in order to set his Promethean creativity free.

For his fourth trial, King Eurystheus sent Hercules back to the same mountainous area, instructing him to perform a deed of the same kind. This time he had to capture a wonderful deer with golden antlers, an animal sacred to Artemis, the goddess of Arcadia. The deer was incredibly swift, and Hercules had to chase it for a whole year. Some say that the hunt went as far north as the holy land of Hyperborea, where Artemis is said to have been as much at home as her twin brother, Apollo. Back in Arcadia, Hercules could finally capture the deer, but not without wounding it slightly in the leg, which slowed it down somewhat. Exhausted, he carried the deer back to the king.

This swift and sacred magical deer, that wears antlers of unearthly gold as a shining flower halo on its noble head, is an image of certain forces that dwell in the lower regions of the spiritual world. The golden antlers show the nature of the deer as the image of a "spiritual instinct." Among nature's elements gold is the most spiritual and represents the sun's power on earth. In capturing the deer, Hercules passes a boundary and comes into contact with new spiritual entities that he must master. No physical danger is involved, only the courage and perseverance never to let up when pursuing spiritual truth. Relentless attempts to snatch or "comprehend" a spiritual truth strengthen the thinking power and result in making incidental contacts with it. These thinking contacts slow the elusive, sacred deer by slightly

---

3. Examples of snow as an image of pure thinking are to be found in the Parsifal saga, as well as in such fairy tales as Grimm's "Mother Holle," and "The Juniper Tree."

wounding it. The hunter is a common image of cool thinking, a power that wounds and lames the instincts (compare Grimm's fairy tales "Little Red-Cap" and "Brother and Sister").

Around Lake Stymphalus, somewhat closer to Mycenae than the site of the two preceding labors, were bird-infested woods, which Hercules was now sent to clean up. An enormous number of huge predatory birds in this region threatened the inhabitants. The monsters were covered with metallic feathers, some of which they shot as arrows at any object below them on earth. They were also extremely gluttonous. In the performance of his labor, Hercules was aided by a divine being. The goddess Athena helped him scare the birds into flight with a big bronze rattle. He then shot as many of them as he could and chased the rest away, never to return again.

The divine help needed in the performance of this labor comes as a direct inspiration from the goddess of wisdom herself. Hercules has to overcome the voracity of his senses and the impatience of his thinking at this early stage of his development. Predatory, soaring birds, clad in a horny, dry body armor, equipped with cruel eyes of incredible intensity, and a tearing beak and merciless talons, depict the predatory tendencies of the human soul, insofar as it lives in the senses and in sense-bound thinking. At this stage of his inner development, the hero must strongly reduce the activities of his senses, of his curiosity, and the compulsion to rush to conclusions.

The last of Hercules' Peloponnesian labors was of a totally different nature. He was sent to Augeas, a gentleman farmer and former Argonaut who ruled the country of Elis, west of Arcadia. It was Hercules' task to clean out the vast cow barns of Augeas, which had never been cleaned before, and to perform this enormous work within one day. It seemed at first a rather domestic duty and one not in keeping with Hercules' semidivine personality. According to some sources, Hercules did not consider this task heroic and requested a reward before starting it. He was promised some cattle, but never received any from Augeas, which led to a battle later on. Hercules, who had been a cowherd when young, fulfilled this impossible task by harnessing the strength of a river. He swiftly dug and scraped a channel from the stables to the river, and the powerful stream of water washed away all the dung.

In this labor he cleanses himself from all the residue of his former earthly and strongly physical life. It is a purification by water, comparable to a baptism.

In the next stretch of his path of development Hercules embarked on a veritable odyssey. He first went south to Crete, then northeast to Thrace, then east to the Asian coast of the Black Sea. The first half of his voyage away from home—labors seven, eight, and nine—led in an easterly direction, to the areas where lie the roots of Aegean culture.

To capture a sacred bull, Hercules was sent by boat to Crete, the former center of the old Minoan culture. The bull, a present from the god Poseidon, was the same one that had fathered the Minotaur, and was now running wild all over the island. It was not hard for Hercules, who had grown up as a cattle herder, to overcome the powerful beast and even ride on its back to the sea. He took it by boat to Mycenae where the king saw it but did not express any interest. Hercules then let it go free. It ran wild in Attica where it became known as the bull of Marathon.

Prepared by the Augean purification, Hercules takes on the majestic lord of sexuality and makes him subject to his willpower, so that he can ride and steer him without making him into an ox.

In Thrace, on the northern shore of the Aegean Sea, there lived a tribe of horse-riding warriors. Their king, Diomedes, possessed a herd of wild, man-eating mares that terrorized the country and bred increasing numbers of war horses. King Eurystheus wanted Hercules to obtain these dangerous animals for him.

On his way there, Hercules performed a very important deed. In passing through Thessaly, in northern Greece, he stayed at the palace of his friend King Admetus. There he learned that Alcestis, the wife of his host, had just died. Hercules wanted to help. He had never been afraid of the angel of death, Thanatos, and he went out to find him. Thanatos was still lingering near the queen's newly closed tomb. The hero wrestled with him until he gave up his prey. Then Hercules was happy and proud to bring Queen Alcestis back to her husband, alive.

After this episode, he continued his long journey on foot until he arrived at the court of King Diomedes. Soon he found a way to tame the carnivorous mares: he took the king prisoner and fed him to his own mares. In this way their evil power was destroyed, and they became tame enough to be driven to Mycenae. In the performance of this labor, Hercules used a device that he also had employed in dealing with the Nemean lion whose skin he removed with the help of its own claws: he turned the destructive power back upon the destroyer. Already at the beginning of his life he had done this when, still an infant, he choked the strangler snakes.

After overcoming the abdominal forces, the bull of Crete in the South, the hero now has to go to the cool head forces in the North. Horses, from Pegasus, the inspirer of "winged words," to the differently colored ones in the Apocalypse, often depict powers of judgment and thinking. One could also think of the speaking horse, Fallada, in the fairy tale, and of the wise horses of the knights in medieval battles who added their own judgment to that of their masters. In this framework, man-eating brood mares are the image of destructive thinking; in other words, the image of doubting. Hercules overcomes this tendency within himself by making the horses destroy their master. He applies doubtful thinking to doubt itself, which destroys the existence of doubt.

When he returned from the North with the horses of Diomedes, Hercules was sent out again. This time at the request of King Eurystheus' daughter, who wanted the girdle that belonged to Hippolyte, the queen of the Amazons. Since the Amazons were a warrior tribe of unmarried women, this famous girdle must have been a piece of body armor. The Amazons lived in a country on the southern shore of the Black Sea in Asia Minor. After a long voyage, Hercules landed among the warlike maidens. They received him kindly, not taking him for an ordinary man, whom they would have killed immediately. Queen Hippolyte was not at all unwilling to give the hero what he came to ask. But all of a sudden, confusion arose. Hera, always alert to what Hercules was doing, made the Amazons think that he was dishonest and that his friendliness towards their queen was the beginning of an attempt to kidnap her. The goddess stirred them into a riot. When the wild horde of screaming warrior maidens bore down upon him, Hercules drew his sword in defense and fought his way back to his waiting ship. During the fighting, the queen was accidentally killed.

This is a trial of Hercules' emotional life, which he has to perform at the request of his princess, not of his king. The princess wanted to be adorned as an Amazon queen. Although Hercules succeeds in providing the princess with what she wanted, he does not withstand this trial very well. Hera was able to confuse him so that he loses his wits, becomes insecure, and for the second time in his life, kills a woman. In his emotional development, Hercules still has a long way to go.

This third group of trials, against the bull, the horses, and the Amazons, uses the macro-microcosmical image of the land-

enclosed sea as a representation of the human body. This is understandable coming from a seafaring people living at the stage of mythopoetic thinking. The image of man appears, as it were, to be kneeling in Egypt; its abdomen in Crete; its head in the Thracian mountains; and its heart, the region of the outstretched arms, on the south shore of the Black Sea. These three trials as a group lead Hercules through developmental processes which take place in the three main streams of his soul processes: his desires (abdomen), thoughts (head), and feelings (heart).

The final group of three labors took Hercules to the West, to the regions where the sun disappears every night. There, at the edge of earth's disk, on the bank of the river Ocean, one finds the main entrances to the netherworld. This world, beyond the boundaries of the physical earth, is the realm of the dead, that is of the spirits.

For his tenth labor, Hercules was sent out by Eurystheus to what he thought to be a land of no return located in the Far West. There he had to steal the cows of a triple-bodied giant and bring them back to Mycenae. This journey was so long that on the way the hero became engaged in all sorts of incidental deeds. He traveled overland all the way through North Africa. His first important encounter took place in Egypt with King Busiris, who made a practice of sacrificing strangers to his gods. When he tried to have this done to Hercules, the hero reversed their roles and sacrificed the king to his own gods, thus paying him in kind. Shortly afterwards, in Libya, he came upon a giant by the name of Antaeus, a son of Gaea who fought all comers to the death. Because Antaeus never seemed to lose any of his strength, Hercules became engaged in a fight without end. Finally, the hero discovered that his opponent derived his abundant forces from contacts with the Earth, his mother. So, just as he had done to the Nemean lion, he lifted the giant off the ground, pressed him against his chest and squeezed him to death. Later, on his way through the hot sands of the desert along the coast of the Mediterranean Sea, the powerful rays of the sun began to bother him. Putting an arrow to his bow, he shot at the sun god who hastened to make friends by promising him the use of his enormous golden bowl, in which he floated each night around half the earth on the river Ocean back to his rising point in the East. Helios, the sun god, who sees and knows all things, realized that Hercules would need means to transport the captured cattle back to the world of men.

When Hercules finally arrived at the bank of the river Ocean, he set up two piles of rocks on both sides of the strait, now called the Strait of Gibraltar. They became known as the Pillars of Hercules, stretching from the mountain Jebel-al-Tarik, at the southern tip of Spain, to the peak called Jebel Musa in the North African Atlas mountains. The giant, whose cattle Hercules had been sent out to steal, lived on an island across the river Ocean, that is, outside the physical world as we know it. The name of this island was Erytheia, meaning "red island" or "island of the sunset." The giant, who had three heads, three sets of arms, and three torsos, supported by one enormous pair of legs, was called Geryon. He was a grandson of Medusa and Poseidon, and therefore an Atlantean.

When he came to the island, Hercules had little trouble eliminating the giant's herdsman and his two-headed dog Orthrus. Another cowherd, who was grazing the cattle of Hades nearby, told Geryon what had happened. The giant went after Hercules, who was already busy driving his cattle away. After a short fight, Geryon was pierced to death by an arrow. Hercules loaded all the cattle into the sun's golden bowl and crossed over to Spain. From the coast he traveled through Spain, southern France and, after crossing the Alps, all the way through Italy. With what was left of the sacred cows, the hero crossed by boat to Greece. Then he walked them to Mycenae.

Hercules' development is now far enough on its way for him to make an attempt to approach the spiritual world. This is a long journey, its length illustrated by the many incidental deeds he performs on the way. One notices the recurrence of a "homeopathic" motif of paying in kind, which to an extent, is Hercules' signature. Also, the wicked, inhospitable king, and the strangling above ground are well-known Herculean motifs. The Antaeus episode brings back to the hero, as he begins the end phase of his path of initiation, the very first labor that he performed. It shows clearly that it was necessary for Hercules to overcome his dependence on physical, earthly forces at this stage. His rather irreverent attitude towards the Titan Helios shows the degree to which he felt familiar with the gods. Arriving at the edge of the physical world, Hercules set up two markers as guiding posts for his reentry after his visit across the river Ocean. On the island of the sunset, the hero had to fight the powers of death. Geryon is closely associated with Hades: both have their cattle grazing closely together, while his shepherd's two-headed dog, Orthrus, is

81

a brother of the hellhound Cerberus, who is three-headed like the giant Geryon. Both dogs, just as the Sphinx, the Nemean lion, and the Hydra of Lerna, are supersensible beings sprung from Typhon and Echidna.

After fighting primordial monsters in the immediate vicinity of Hades' realm and overcoming them with ease, Hercules obtains a rich herd of divine cattle, i.e., great spiritual wealth for the king of Mycenae. To cross the river Ocean on his way out, Hercules must have used a vessel, though no tradition mentions it. This vessel undergoes a metamorphosis while the hero gains access to the sacred wealth, and becomes the enormous golden bowl of the radiating sun. His ensuing extensive travels caused the memory of Hercules to linger throughout the entire western part of the Mediterranean. In this labor, Hercules came as close as possible to entering the realm of the spirit. It is the last stage in his preparation to becoming an initiate.

When he had proved his ability to penetrate the far western regions and return alive, Eurystheus wanted Hercules to go there again, this time to approach the very threshold of the spirit world. He now sent him on a mission to enter the realms of Hades. To show that he had been there, he had to bring back alive the dreaded watchdog Cerberus, the guardian at the gate of the netherworld. In this, the most profound trial on his path of development, Hercules secured the help and guidance of the gods Athena and Hermes. They showed him the path deep into the earth, which is at the same time the path deep into one's self. There he met the awesome god Hades who, amazed to see a human being not yet dead within his realm, gave him permission to carry off the hellhound, provided he would do so unarmed and that he would bring him back. When Hercules came closer to the entrance of the palace he found the hero Theseus sitting in the chair of forgetfulness, unable to stand up, and not aware of where he was. In gratitude for the friendship the Athenian hero had shown him during a time of great need, Hercules wrenched him loose, and set him free. Then he approached Cerberus. This enormous doglike being had long hair made up of thin, living snakes. It had three fierce heads, growling and clicking their teeth. Protected by his lion mantle, Hercules lifted the monster bodily off the ground and held it high above his head. Proudly he carried it all the way up to the world of men and to the palace of the Mycenaean king. Eurystheus all but fainted at the awesome sight, and told the hero to carry the beast back, immediately!

To come into contact with the spirit world, a threshold has to be passed which is guarded by a threefold supersensible being. The same being, which is depicted in this myth as the three-headed hound, appears in the Oedipus story as the Sphinx, a threefold composite of man, lion, and eagle. Man, who is a threefold being, confronts himself in this situation seeing, as in a mirror, a monstrous caricature. If he can overcome his fear of his own being by gradually making the component forces of his soul, his thinking, his feeling, and that which underlies the performance of his acts, pure in themselves and harmoniously unified with each other, their mirror image will no longer be threatening or grotesque. Then he will have become strong enough to pass unharmed through the gate leading into the spiritual world. He will be able to enter, while still in the body, the realm in which noninitiates can only find themselves after death. Through his deed Hercules shows that the guardian of the threshold could be moved, and so makes it possible for other initiates to follow his example.

Before starting on his last labor Hercules went through a year of preparation at Eleusis, a holy place not far from Athens. Here he trained under the guidance and with the instruction of priests in the mysteries of Demeter and Persephone, and of Dionysus. When his year was completed, he confirmed his status as an initiate by undergoing the rituals of the Eleusian initiation, under the direction of Theseus.

Then, accompanied by Chiron, the wisest of all centaurs, who greatly suffered from his wound, he set out on his journey. This took him along the edge of the ancient world. First he went to the East, to the border of Europe and Asia, where in the Caucasus he came upon Prometheus, still standing there, chained to the mountain. Overcome by pity for his suffering, Hercules killed the voracious vulture which daily gnawed Prometheus' liver. Chiron then laid down his life on behalf of the protector and inspirator of mankind, and Prometheus, the Titan, became free again. From the Caucasus, Hercules traveled across Asia Minor toward Egypt. Then on again he went through North Africa, performing many deeds of capturing and killing, until he arrived at the western shore. He went somewhere beyond the Pillars which he had piled up on the occasion of his first visit to the West. Here was the garden of the gods, in which grew the tree with golden apples. This wonderful tree had been a wedding present from Mother Earth to Zeus and Hera. There was a snake or dragon at its foot whose task it was to guard it. These images are akin to those of the Hebrew myth of paradise with its tree of life, and the snake entwined in it. Hesperides, whose name means "nymphs of the West," or "daughters of the evening star," were entrusted with the guardianship of this garden, also called the Elysium.

It was Hercules' mission to take the golden apples, the food of immortality, from the tree of life and bring them back to the king. According to one tradition, he went straight up to the dragon, killed the monster, and gathered the apples from the tree. Other sources tell a more elaborate version. They say that on arrival in the West, Hercules did not know where to look for the garden of the Hesperides; actually only gods were allowed to enter this garden. He therefore went to the father of the nymphs, to Atlas, who was standing nearby bearing the vault of heaven on his shoulders. He offered to relieve him of his task for the time the Titan would need to gather the apples for him. Atlas was very eager to do this for him, and soon came back with the heavenly fruit. Mindful perhaps of the recent liberation of his brother, Prometheus, Atlas suggested that Hercules should become his substitute, and he would take the apples to Eurystheus for him. Showing unusual cunning, Hercules pretended to go along with this plan. But first he asked Atlas to take over his former burden for a few moments, so that he could arrange a pad over his shoulders. Atlas fell for this trick, and Hercules left him there to continue the task assigned him. When Hercules gave Eurystheus the magic apples, the king did not know what to do with them, so Hercules gave them to the goddess Athena.

In this twelfth and last of his labors, Hercules shows the powers of an initiate. He performs deeds important for all mankind by freeing the Titan forces in East and West. He delivers Prometheus from his punishment so that his great creative force and his great love for human beings could again work in the world. He sets Atlas free for a short time by taking over, as a tower of strength, his titanic task of bearing the vault of heaven. Now, from the garden of the gods the golden (i.e., spiritual) life-giving fruits could be given mankind. However, mankind, represented by Eurystheus, is not yet ready enough to receive them. Therefore, the hero gives them to the goddess of wisdom, Athena, to keep for mankind. She could give them to later generations, when these, according to her divine judgment, would be able to make good use of them.

Now that all of Hercules' sins were expiated, Eurystheus set him free. However, in spite of his initiation, Hercules was sometimes overwhelmed by his desires. The story tells that once he fought a bull and broke off one of its horns in subduing it. This bull was the disguise taken by the river god Achelous in order to fight Hercules, who wanted to marry the Princess Deianira, with whom Achelous, too, was in love. He overcame the river god and married beautiful Deianira. *This little myth deals with Hercules' initiation. After succeeding in dominating the bull, i.e., his instincts, he is able to unite himself with his own spiritual being in complete identification, as with a royal bride.* Hercules departed with his princess; and before they had gone far, they came upon a river they wanted to cross. There, a ferryman, a centaur called Nessus, would gallop through the water carrying the passengers on his back. Hercules expected to be tall enough to make the crossing on foot, and went on without his new wife. Deianira mounted the centaur when Hercules was already at the other side. Suddenly, Nessus turned downstream in the middle of the river, and ran away with the terrified princess. Within a minute he was shot with a poisonous arrow. *After initiation, the hero's newly found spiritual being is still tender and unprotected in the world. In the first, still transitional phase (when she is carried across a river), she can easily be waylaid and offended by powerful instincts (centaur) when left alone with them.* Nessus stumbled to the bank of the river and told Deianira with his dying voice to collect some of his blood and some of his sperm in a vial. She should perfume Hercules clothes with it whenever she wanted to prevent him from being unfaithful to her. Nessus died just before Hercules reached him. He saw the centaur's soul depart from his body in a birdlike form.

Hercules and Deianira were happy together and had many children. The little vial with centaur blood was all but forgotten. Still, Hercules could act wildly sometimes. For the senseless murder of a young man, Zeus punished him by having him sold as a slave in Asia Minor. He was bought in the market of Lydia's capital city by Omphale, the queen of that country. The queen made his life very hard by ordering him to do the work of a servant girl, and demanding that in doing so he should wear her dress, while she walked about in his lionskin.

Since Lydia is not far from the country of the Amazons, it looks as if Hercules here had to complete what he did not accomplish in his ninth labor. By playing the role of a woman, he has to identify himself with his emotional life, which in myth is commonly depicted as a woman.

Free after a year, he went to war and was victorious in different battles, after which he traveled homeward with booty and prisoners. Among the latter were several beautiful princesses. A messenger was sent forward to announce to Deianira that her husband was on his way home. This messenger did not fail to mention the graceful princesses. Deianira now thought of her little vial. She took a beautiful garment, which during his absence she had woven for her husband as a homecoming present and sprinkled it with the centaur's blood. Hercules was happy with the present his wife had made for him with such loving thoughtfulness. But as soon as he put it on, it began to burn him. Try as he might, he could not strip it off his arms and back. In a panic of pain he ran away to the mountains. On Mount Oeta, he made himself a funeral pyre, mounted it, and entreated all onlookers to light it. No one was willing to do anything but look. Finally, a stranger, a shepherd who happened to pass, did not mind putting fire to it. In gratitude, Hercules gave him his bow and arrows. Soon the smoke was rising into the air and rendering the hero invisible. As an answer to the smoke a cloud approached from above, and enveloped the top of the mountain. A majestic burst of thunder echoed through the valleys, when the demigod entered heaven.

In a fire of purification all the parts of his being that had been in touch with his centauric nature, i.e., all his mortal parts, are burned away. His immortal being becomes free to ascend to heaven, where he is united with his father, Zeus, who grants him eternal life. He also is reconciled with Hera and marries her daughter Hebe, the lovely goddess of youth. He will never age in his eternal life, but remain young and strong like a god.

———

Hercules was the most popular hero of the Greeks. All Greeks considered themselves children of Hercules, from Odysseus at the beginning to Alexander, the great Macedonian, who stands at the end of the Greek development. Every Greek boy wanted to become like Hercules. A winner at the Olympic Games took his name as a title, and was called "a Hercules."

Many Greeks thought that he had been the founder of the Olympic Games, which were the essence of the ancient Greek way of life.

86

JASON
AND THE QUEST FOR THE GOLDEN FLEECE

Man's real being is of a spiritual nature. It lives and works in his soul and in his body, in the wisdom of structure and function, in the power and agility of muscles and bones, in the weaving of blood pulse and breathing. It sleeps in the skill of his motions, moves and dances in dreamlike fashion in the symphonies of his emotional life, and awakens in the stillness of his thinking. In his spirituality, the dignity, the liveliness, and the creativity of man reside. Man's individual reality as a spiritual being is of infinite value both to himself and to the group to which he and his fellow men belong. But animal, instinctual forces can separate man from his spiritual dignity. It happened in the beginning with the Fall of Man. It continues to happen in each individual being while growing up. When the culture of a people loses its spiritual strength, it cannot defend itself against the deadly forces of materialism, and culture disappears, becoming a thing of the past, a memory.

There is a great and secret longing in man to recapture his spiritual dignity and restore it to everyday life. To accomplish this, heroic efforts must be made; fearsome instinctive forces must be tamed and harnessed. Great determination and courage are needed. Divine protection and clear, unfaltering thinking must act as guides. When man succeeds in recovering and revitalizing his spiritual being, a strong healing influence is brought to bear upon the civilization of his group as well as upon the quality of his personal life.

The loss of man's spiritual being and its recovery is depicted in a famous myth, "The Quest for the Golden Fleece." The first part of the myth tells how the bearer of the Golden Fleece, a sacred ram, appeared in Greece, and then departed to the East, to another country where the people worshiped it. In a second episode, we meet the hero who is going to fetch the lost treasure and bring it back to his people. The third story recounts the adventures of the expedition sent out to the East; the fourth depicts the heroic deeds that had to be performed to capture the Golden Fleece. The final episode tells of the adventures on the return voyage.

Orchomenus, the old Boeotian town near Thebes, is the scene of action for the first myth. Its inhabitants originally lived more to the north in Thessaly. The story begins in the manner of a fairy tale.

"There was once a king and a queen, who had two children. The king's name was Athamas, and his queen was called Nephele, their children were Prince Phrixus and Princess Helle . . ." However, before the story has a chance to unfold between these four characters, we learn that Athamas repudiated Nephele, the friendly mother of his children—Nephele means "cloud"—and instead married Ino, "the strong one." With the appearance of this typical stepmother, evil forces enter. Ino belonged to the first family of Boeotia. Her father was Cadmus, the Syrian founder of Thebes, and brother of Europa, the mother of King Minos of Crete. The tragic character of Ino's family shows itself in the fate of her three sisters. Semele, the mother of Dionysus, was killed by fire, when at her request her lover, Zeus, appeared to her undisguised in his divine form. Agave, a bacchante, killed her own son, Pentheus, in a Dionysian frenzy, thinking that he was a lion; and Autonoë's only son was killed by his own hunting dogs after Artemis had changed him into a deer. This was his punishment for innocently violating the privacy of the hunter goddess when she was bathing in a mountain lake. Dionysian forces were strong in Ino's family, and the killing of sons had already taken place. As is typical for the stepmother in a folktale, Ino was afraid that her own future children would be subordinate to the son of her husband's first marriage. For this reason she planned to eliminate the crown prince.

The queen, as mother of the king's children, is at the same time the mother of his people. Therefore it is her task to care for the feeding of the tribe. The new queen, Ino, was not the real mother who had nourished the children with her own milk in infancy. She was a stepmother to whom the food of the tribe was not a sacred substance. She did not hesitate to use it for the sake of her own egotistic devices.

Ino had all the grain stored for the coming year's sowing roasted in an oven to kill its germinal power. The next year, to the despair and bewilderment of the people, no crop came up. When starvation became imminent, King Athamas sent an envoy to Delphi for advice. On his return the messenger was intercepted by the queen, who bribed him to declare that the oracle had advised to kill and sacrifice Prince Phrixus in order to restore the fertility of the land. The people understood the sense of this ritual. The sacrifice of the king's seed, his son, would induce the gods to restore the life powers of the seed grain. The king was horrified, but his starving people forced him to consent. Just as in later days Agamemnon would be forced to sacrifice his daughter Iphigenia on the altar for the sake of the people, so Athamas gave up his beloved eldest son.

However, Nephele, the real mother of Phrixus, knew about the terrible danger. With great fervor she prayed to the god Hermes, who comforted her. On the day appointed for the sacrifice, he came to her aid and invisibly watched the procedures. When the young prince had been ritually prepared and was lying down on the altar awaiting the priest's knife, with his twin sister standing nearby, her eyes full of tears, and all the people looking on in sadness, the god suddenly made a celestial, golden-haired ram appear in front of the altar. With great presence of mind, the prince and the princess, charmed by its golden shine, climbed on the ram's back. Then, like a meteor, the majestic animal flew through the air and disappeared in an easterly direction before the incredulous eyes of everyone. In these moments of extreme concentration and awe, Hermes, the leader of souls, made everyone momentarily clairvoyant, so they could perceive the children's and their tribe's spiritual being in its golden aura. The ram flew east across the Aegean Sea. Just before they arrived at the other side, Princess Helle, sitting behind her brother's back, slipped and drowned in the narrow strait, named after her, the Hellespont. Phrixus went on alone all over Asia Minor until, in view of the mighty Caucasus mountains, he landed on the shore of the Black Sea in remote Colchis. Here Phrixus—who on the way had lost his emotional attachment to his people (his sister)—was inspired by Hermes to sacrifice the great ram to Zeus and to offer its Golden Fleece to Aeëtes, king of the fierce Colchidians. The king was greatly pleased with this magic present. He hung the Golden Fleece on the trunk of a huge oak tree which grew straight up in a sacred grove close to the sea. At its foot an enormous dragon installed itself to guard the golden treasure. Now the sacrifice of Phrixus was completed in a way different from his stepmother's intention. He was absorbed into this non-Greek tribe when he married the king's oldest daughter, Chalciope. A few years later, he died after the birth of his son, Argus, without, however, obtaining a

89

proper burial.

With the eastward flight of Phrixus and his golden-haired ram to the country of Colchis, we arrive at the edge of a very ancient pre-European culture near the Caucasus mountains. Aeëtes, who appears in the role of a king in this myth, was a son of the sun god, and himself a god of the wind, as his name indicates. The myth tells us that both his sister, Circe, and his daughter, Medea, were powerful magicians who could cast spells and perform incantations which worked through the power of their words. We also learn that he was the owner of fire-breathing beasts, both bulls and dragons. The god of the wind, i.e., of the external, organized air in the macrocosmos, is at the same time the god of the air, which human beings organize within their throats and mouths to form language.

This Aeëtes, god of the wind and of breathing, appears in Germanic mythology under the name Wotan, god of the raging storm,[1] and in Iceland as Odin, god of breath and of the power of language. In the old Icelandic tradition, there are important tree imaginations, remnants of a much older mystery religion. Odin offered a part of his divine breath to two trees growing in a paradise at the seashore. This gave them an inner life. The ash tree, Askr, became the first man; the elm tree, Embla, the first woman. The whole threefold world of gods, men, and giants was conceived as being located on and in an archetypal ash tree, called Yggdrasill. In the course of his own development, for gods, too, mature, Odin once hung by his hair on the "windy" world tree and in his suffering invented the human language. Images of two trees at the beginning of creation are also found in the Hebrew tradition, in Genesis, the first book of the Old Testament. Here, however, the trees, the one of life, and the other of the knowledge of good and evil, are not images of human beings. At the corners of the former Atlantean world, in the Caucasus and in Iceland, we find reminiscences of extremely ancient imaginations regarding the origin and the being of man. The uprightness of his skeleton with spine, arms with hands, legs with feet, is imaged as a tree. This produces an idea of man as a spinal, not yet as a cerebral being. On Iceland, the being of man, in the person of his creator Odin, hangs in the uprightness of the tree (skeleton), and in this position

---

1. Compare the German, wüten, "to rage": Wednesday is named after Woden, i.e., Wotan.

is inspired to the invention of speech, a uniquely human achievement.

At the foot of the Caucasus, the people of Colchis also knew the tree of man. It grew in a grove sacred to the war god, and carried man's spirituality as a "golden fleece" hung on its upright trunk. Like the Icelandic world ash, this eastern tree had at its foot a fierce, destructive dragon. The Icelandic dragon, however, was not there to defend the tree, but with its brood it gnawed the roots of Yggdrasill.

With the retreat of man's spirituality into its original homeland, paradise, and the loss of the royal children, a time of barbarism descended on the land of Orchomenus and its environs. Spiritual culture disappeared. For a long time the stepmotherly forces held sway in greed and lust for power. Some twenty years later, during the next generation of men, the cultural life of Greece was still in darkness.

Athamas and Ino were still reigning in Orchomenus, while to the north of them in Thessaly, their parent country, a wicked ruler, called Pelias ("the black one"), had usurped the throne of his brother Aeson, the rightful king in the city of Iolcus. When this happened, Aeson's son, Diomedes, was still very young. The king, taken by surprise, was put in prison with his family. His only hope was that his son would one day be able to remedy the disastrous situation of the royal family. He therefore had trusted servants take the young prince to a secret area in the mountains. There, in a cave, he grew up in the good care of the wise centaur Chiron, the famous tutor of heroes. Chiron gave Diomedes a thorough training in the martial arts as well as in music. In addition, the boy learned to know the nature of man, of animals, and of plants. In this way, he gradually became fully at home in the realm of the forces of life and healing. Chiron was proud of him and gave him a new name: Jason, "the healer."

When he had completed his education, Jason took leave of his noble teacher and set out to find his way back home, so that he could set his father free. He was now in the prime of his youth and, wearing a leopard skin, looked like a handsome young Hercules. On the way he came to the bank of the river Anaurus. An old woman was standing there, waiting for an opportunity to go to the other side. Jason offered to carry her across on his back. Strangely, during the crossing the frail old lady became so heavy that Jason's staggering feet sank deeper and deeper into the muddy bottom of the stream. When one of his sandals became stuck, he could not retrieve it. Exhausted, he reached the other bank on one sandal and one bare foot. The old woman thanked him in a friendly but very dignified way and revealed that she was not a mere mortal woman, but the goddess Hera herself who had wanted to test his powers and who promised that from now on she would always be on his side. *Such behavior is characteristic of Hera, the goddess of conservation. She always supports the legitimate ruler.*

Like most heroes, Jason grows up away from his father's influence, so that he is able to prepare himself for the life of a true individual. Coming out of the highlands of his childhood, he crosses the boundary river to reach the coastal plain of his father's realm where he intends to live his adult life. Hera protects him at the river crossing. She marks this transition for him by causing him to lose one of his sandals and then making herself known to him in disguise. With one foot well shod he stands in the world of adults; with the other foot still bare he is a child of nature.

Jason entered the gate of Iolcus, the ancient Thessalian harbor town on the bay of Pagasae, where his father's palace stood. His wicked uncle Pelias, by now an old man, was still living there. Jason's presence in the town was soon noticed. People stopped to stare at the handsome young stranger, the very image of health, strength, and innocence. Speculations and wishful thinking arose on all sides. It did not take long for the rumors to reach the ear of the king. Pelias became very nervous, for the oracle of Zeus in Dodona had warned him to watch out for a stranger who would come into town wearing only one sandal. Jason was summoned to the palace. Without any wavering or fear, he told his uncle who he was and that the had come to take over the throne and scepter of the country which rightly belonged to his father. Pelias pretended to accept this nephew as the new king, his successor. But first he delegated him to fulfill an all-important mission on behalf of the people, as his representative. The spirit of Phrixus, he told him, often appeared to him in dreams and haunted him, demanding that the Golden Fleece should be brought back to Greece where it belonged, together with his dead body, which had not been properly buried. King Pelias himself was too old for such a strenuous task. He considered himself fortunate that Jason had come, because now he had a successor who could start this difficult task in his stead. When he returned with his mission fulfilled, the king would be glad to give the kingdom into the hands of such a courageous young prince who had proved himself able to perform great deeds.

Although the goddess Hera was not at all in favor of King Pelias, the task he set for Jason was to her liking. She inspired and encouraged the young hero to start organizing the expedition. He needed a good ship and a crew. Jason sent out heralds in all directions to recruit the heroes of Greece. There was a great response. From everywhere heroes traveled to Iolcus to help prepare the crusade. The ship was built by Argus, a son of Phrixus, and a shipwright by profession, who was happy to help secure his dead father's rest by bringing his body back for proper interment. The ship was named Argo, after its builder. Argus made it large enough for fifty oarsmen. The goddess of wisdom, Athena, who usually sides with Hera in her wish to restore important traditions, acquired permission from her father, Zeus, to cut a piece from the sacred oak at Dodona. She helped fit it as a beam in the prow of the Argo, so that the ship would tell the sailors, or "Argonauts," where to go. Among the crew members were all the well-known heroes of the generation before the Trojan war, such as Acastus, a son of Pelias; Admetus and Augeas, who play a role in the Hercules myth; Hercules himself with his attendant Hylas; Argus the shipwright; Calaïs and Zetes, the winged sons of the North Wind; Castor and Polydeuces (son of Zeus); Laertes, the father of Odysseus; Oileus, father of Ajax; Peleus, father of Achilles; Orpheus, the great singer; Jason, the leader of them all, and 36 others. When Hercules, after capturing the wild boar of Erymanthos, joined the Argonauts, they all took it for granted that he should be the commander of the expedition. Hercules, however, was not too proud to serve under Jason.

After performing the customary sacrifices and rituals, the young commander took the ship out of the bay of Pagasae, where it had been built. Orpheus played his magical music to which all the heroes rowed in strong and harmonious rhythm. After rounding the cape, they set sail in a northeasterly direction and arrived in due time at the harbor town of Myrina on the large island of Lemnos. Here all the inhabitants were women. They had murdered their husbands to punish them for their adulterous behavior. After some hesitation, and not without a few moments of great tension, the group of all the great heroes of Greece was invited to stay, not only to protect the island against attacks, but also to protect the population from extinction. The Argonauts remained on Lemnos for a whole year, and many children were born to the militant women. A son of Jason himself later became king of Lemnos. It was Hercules who at last grew impatient. One night he knocked on all the houses and forced his comrades back on board ship. They set sail that evening and continued in the original direction until they arrived at the holy island of Samothrace, a center of ancient religion. In the temple cave they all underwent a ritual initiation, and, in addition, the blessing of the mystery gods, the Cabiri, was bestowed on them for a safe voyage.

Sailing on from Samothrace they made a course change of ninety degrees southeast. After some time they resumed their original direction and secretly entered the Strait of Hellespont. They slipped through at night, fortunate that nobody on the Trojan guardships noticed them in the dark. In the course of that night, Argus offered a libation to the spirit of his father's twin sister Helle, who had drowned at this spot as she fell from the golden ram's back. Sailing into the Propontis, the entrance hall of the Black Sea, they landed at Bear Island, and were welcomed by King Cyzicus with a banquet and festivities. It happened to be his wedding day. From there on they again followed their original direction en route to the Bosporus. Because of a terrible wind, Jason gave the helmsman permission to turn back in the night. They landed not knowing where, and were immediately attacked by natives. In the morning they saw that they had come back to Bear Island, and that King Cyzicus and many of his men had been slain in the night's battle. In honor of Cyzicus, they held funeral games and, after placating the local gods, sailed on toward the Bosporus.

The arrival in Iolcus of the innocent hero who, as his name indicates, is destined to be the healer of his people, electrifies all the heroes in Greece. The leading personages of Greek culture join hands to retrieve the former spiritual strength of their people. Their vehicle bears the blessing of Zeus, incorporated in the wood from Dodona. Their expedition is sponsored by Hera and watched over by Athena. All crewmen obey Jason's command. He thinks for them in making plans; they belong to him and carry out his will. Jason, the healer, is on his way toward spirit land, his body a magic ship and his soul forces working as heroic soldiers and sailors. The voyage proceeds from trial to trial. The first test is of an emotional nature. During a whole year they live in luxury with the women of Lemnos. If it had not been for the authority of Hercules, Jason's great example, he might have given up the expedition and stayed on the island for the rest of his life. Back on course, Jason receives the special blessing of the ancient mystery gods on Samothrace. This rekindles his enthusiasm for the task he has taken upon himself. Then the Argo makes the turn which sets it again on its course. Silently, they row through dangerous narrows, feeling great relief when they enter the wide Propontis where they enjoy some respite. Suddenly the ship is pushed back and their progress hindered. Jason does not persevere, but lets himself become overwhelmed. He loses his momentum and his direction, and unwittingly kills his former host in the dark. Fear and lack of perseverance make him retrace his route to a point he had previously left, where the circumstances are no longer right for him. The original hospitality changes to hostility, and Jason loses a good friend and defender.

Continuing on their way to the Bosporus, the Argonauts engaged in a rowing contest. Jason and Hercules held out longer than anyone else, until Jason nearly fainted, which happened at the same moment Hercules broke his oar. The Argo was beached. While everyone was occupied preparing food, Hercules went to find a good tree out of which to make a new oar. His dear friend and shield bearer, Hylas, went with him part of the way, but then turned in the direction of a spring to fetch water. He never returned again. The nymphs of the spring had fallen in love with the handsome boy and drawn him under water so that he might stay with them. The whole night long Hercules searched for him. At dawn neither of them had come back. Jason had no choice. With a favorable wind blowing, and all the heroes shouting the name of Hercules, the Argo set sail toward the northeast. Again, they landed on an island. The local king, Amycus, a son of Poseidon, was a proud boxer and liked to challenge all strangers to a fight to the death, which he invariably won. Polydeuces, the old Greek champion, who years ago had taught Hercules the art of boxing, accepted the challenge, and after a terrible fight, succeeded in killing the king. The islanders became hostile, but they were routed and their city destroyed. Jason sacrificed twenty red bulls from the booty as a peace offering to Poseidon to make amends to the god for the loss of his son, Amycus.

The last adventure of the Argonauts before entering the Black Sea took place on the northern shore where Jason, with some members of the crew, marched far to visit the blind King Phineus. Because Phineus had the gift of looking into the future, he had often thwarted the plans of Zeus, and for this the god had made him blind. As an additional punishment he had to suffer daily visits of the Harpies, predatory birds with women's faces, who grasped his food from the table and spread a loathsome stench over everything. Jason was eager to ask the seer's advice and promised that as a reward he would deliver him from the evil birds. When the table was set, and the two arrogant monsters appeared, all the Argonauts drew their swords, but could not touch the Harpies as they continually flew out of reach. Then Zetes and Calaïs, who as sons of the North Wind were equipped with wings, sprang high up into the air and attacked the birdwomen from above. This attack from an unexpected direction took them by surprise and they sped away. All the heroes saw them disappear toward the west with Zetes and Calaïs in hot pursuit. Jason described to Phineus all that was taking place. When the sons of the North Wind had come so close to the squeaking black birds that they were ready to draw their swords, they saw their own shadows cast on the dense clouds ahead. Suddenly a rainbow arched through the sky and at its end appeared the goddess Iris, messenger of Zeus. She told them that Zeus did not want his Harpies to be killed, and promised they would never come back again to mistreat old King Phineus. The sons of the North Wind made a leisurely turn and calmly flew back to the other Argonauts, while the Harpies raced on towards the west. The blind king now explained to Jason how to navigate his ship all the way to Colchis and gave him the additional information he needed for the voyage.

The adventures in the Propontis before entering the Black Sea (the Pontus) itself, gives the individual heroes the chance to show what they can do. First, Jason proves to be nearly as strong an oarsman as Hercules, which is a great boost for his self-reliance. Hercules' presence is no longer necessary: his oar is broken. After some private adventures in Asia Minor, Hercules returns to the Peloponnesûs to continue his own development, performing his labors for King Eurystheus. It was the task of King Amycus to keep people from entering the Black Sea after they had succeeded in sailing past the Trojan guards in the Hellespont. He is a primitive guardian of the threshold, placed there by Poseidon to deter people from entering his spiritual realm. In the absence of Hercules, Amycus is eliminated by the older hero Polydeuces. After this the way is free. But Jason first goes to seek advice from the powers of ancient clairvoyance. King Phineus, like Tiresias and other soothsayers, was blind. This is indicative of his seership, of his looking inward upon his mental images instead of outward into the world of sense perceptions. The Harpies, just like the Stymphalian birds, depict the voracity and ruthlessness of sense perception. They were sent by Zeus, the god of clear thinking, to starve Phineus and his atavistic clairvoyance to death. They cannot be destroyed. But our spiritual forces, winged beings, sons of the wind, can chase them away. After the departure of Hercules, Jason is on his own, and on the verge of passing into the Black Sea area, a part of the Eastern world. As Chiron had taught him, he is going to make use of clairvoyance to guide him to his goal.

At the entrance of the Bosporus two rocks, the Symplegades, stood on either side of the fairway. Between them, the waters came rushing down with great force. Not rooted in the sea bottom, they swiveled towards each other and rhythmically drove together with a great clash, demolishing any ship that happened to pass between them. Phineus had informed Jason about them, and upon his advice he had someone stand at the prow of the Argo and send a dove between the rocks. The white bird flew with all its zeal and might, losing only a few tail feathers when the Symplegades thundered together. Jason, with great concentration, had been following the flight of the dove, observing its progress in relation to the rhythm of the rocks' movement. As soon as the Symplegades started to move outward again, the Argo was urged forward with all oarsmen pulling like one man to the stirring rhythm of Orpheus' music. Gathering top speed, the Argo pulled through. Only its stern ornament was scraped off, when the rocks snapped shut behind the ship like the blades of huge scissors. From there on the voyage continued unchallenged and speedily along the southern shore of the Black Sea.

The Argonauts had some minor adventures with local people, lost a few crew members, but gained as replacements four older brothers of Argus, whom they had rescued in a storm. Near a small island, great flocks of birds flew over the Argo and wounded some heroes by dropping their copper feathers upon them, forcing them to wear their helmets. Phineus had warned them about the birds. They now followed his advice and landed in order to chase all the birds away. Shortly before nightfall they arrived at their destination, the land of Colchis at the foot of the Caucasus. They sailed up the Phasis River, made sacrifices to the local gods, and hid the Argo under dense trees in a secluded inlet.

This final obstacle, the Symplegades, is like an entrance gate through which Jason sends his own soul as a probe. By exactly imitating what he had clairvoyantly seen himself do in the form of the white bird, he succeeds in taking the Argo into Poseidon's spiritual waters. He loses nothing but an unnecessary ornament.

The night after their arrival, the Argonauts deliberated their plans. At the same time, in the world of the gods, the real plans were being made. The goddesses Hera, who had sponsored Jason, and Athena, who carefully watched over him, discussed how they could best enable their protégé to obtain the Golden Fleece. They agreed that he would need help from the outside and decided that this should come through the aid of Aphrodite. The goddess of love, slightly amazed but greatly honored by this unexpected request from goddesses who as a rule did not think too kindly of her, promised her help. She went to find her little son Eros[2] and promised him a wonderful present, a golden ball of great beauty, if he would shoot one of his love arrows into the heart of the Princess Medea, the daughter of King Aeëtes, so that she would fall in love with Jason. In this way the Argonauts would acquire a powerful helper within the palace.

Meanwhile Jason and his companions had come to a decision. When they saw the white horses of Aeëtes' father, Helios, come neighing out of their splendid stables on the hill behind the city and draw the sun's chariot up into the morning sky, they set out together to pay the king a visit. Aeëtes, who did not like strangers, was annoyed that they had been able to penetrate into his realm past the Trojan sentinels and the boxer king on his small island. He could not imagine how they could have passed between the clashing rocks. When Jason then stated that the Golden Fleece originally had belonged to his people and that they had come to take it back with them, Aeëtes laughed spitefully. In a harsh voice, he ordered the Argonauts to go back where they came from, and threatened cruel punishment if they did not obey.

Medea was struck by the appearance and the gentle voice of Jason. When he answered her brutish father in a decent and calm manner, the arrow of Eros deeply penetrated her heart, and she made the decision to be of help to this interesting young hero. Even

---

2. Eros, the boy god of romantic love, son of Aphrodite, is a being totally different from the great primordial power of love, which is the real god of creation.

Aeëtes was somewhat impressed by the noble attitude of Jason and his companions. He therefore decided upon a friendly gesture, and promised to give them the Fleece if Jason proved himself worthy of it by performing some incredible deeds. He first had to yoke two fire-breathing bulls to a plow; then, with this team, plow a sacred field in the middle of the town. In the furrows he would have to sow dragon's teeth, which the king would provide. Out of the dragon's teeth, armed men would rise up, and Jason would have to fight them all to the death. If he proved to be able to perform all this, then the king would not mind giving him the fleece. The Argonauts stood like statues, and even Jason looked pale. These tasks were impossible. Without a word they turned around and marched back to their ship. There they sat on the shore under the trees in thought.

In the evening a Colchidian lady approached their camp: Chalciope, the widow of Phrixus. She came to tell Jason that her sister, Princess Medea, loved him with all her heart and that she would make it possible for him to overcome all his trials on condition that he would take her with him on the Argo when he returned to his home. Jason went back with the Lady Chalciope to meet Medea in secret and swore that he would do what she wished. She then gave him a bottle with a powerful medicine and explained its application and effects.

In the morning, in accordance with Medea's instruction, Jason opened the bottle and put the lotion all over his body, his shield, and his weapons. Thus prepared, he again appeared before the king with his retinue of Argonauts. He was led to the stables, and in a sudden silence from the curious bystanders, he was allowed to enter. The heavy door was immediately closed and bolted behind his back. Through the power of Medea's medicine, the fire of the bulls' breathing could not harm the hero. As one who was nearly as strong as Hercules and who, through his training with Chiron, was fully acquainted with the nature of animals, he had no trouble subduing the bulls, making them accept the yoke on their necks and being hitched to the plow. With the strength of his arms and the steady power of his voice, Jason held the snorting bulls in check as he plowed the sacred field with them. It took the whole day to draw the deep, straight furrows over the field of Ares. When he had finished, he took the bulls back to the stables and went to the king to ask for the dragon's teeth. Aeëtes grudingly provided them in the large box in which they had been lying for many years. Jason sowed the teeth at nightfall. When he had finished, the field lay bristling with armed men who had risen, or were still rising from the soil of Ares' field under the light of a full moon. A rock hurled in their midst made them start fighting each other. Medea had alerted him to this, but Jason knew it himself. The same had happened when Cadmus, the founder of Thebes, and the father of Phrixus' stepmother, Ino, had long ago been in a similar situation. As a matter of fact, the teeth which Aeëtes had given Jason came from the same dragon long since dead. When the fighting of the sown men had come to an end, Jason went among them and put the survivors to the sword.

The king was astonished. Not wanting to give up the precious Golden Fleece, he became very angry and threatened to kill all the foreigners and burn their ship. But Medea, who knew her father and was prepared for this situation, already had taken her beloved Jason to the grove of Ares outside the city, where the Golden Fleece hung shining as a light among the dark trees. The enormous dragon lay coiled around the roots of the oak tree, its eyes fixed upon the visitors, the tip of its tail moving nervously. Medea started to hum and sing magic incantations that made the dragon relax and finally fall asleep. While Medea kept her eyes fixed on the dragon, Jason hurried forward and quickly lifted the Fleece from the tree. Then they both hastened to the place where the Argo lay waiting for them. They rushed aboard and the men started rowing with all their strength. The Colchidians attacked them with rocks and with arrows. Many of the Argonauts were wounded. But Medea with her magic medicine healed them all.

Colchis is the region where the realm of the spirit abuts on the physical world in the East.[3] It is the land of the sunrise. The gods mentioned in relation to this country are Helios, the sun god, a Titan; Hecate, the protectress of Medea; Hephaestus, who had built the palace and made the fiery bulls; Ares, the war god, whose field had to be plowed, and in whose sacred grove the Golden Fleece was hanging on an oak tree; Athena, who had given the dragon's teeth to the king; and King Aeëtes, the god of the wind. Another tradition tells that not far from Colchis was the deep cave out of which Hercules appeared with the hellhound Cerberus on his shoulders. The Golden Fleece had been taken back into this part of heaven when the original owners, the Greeks, forfeited it.

---

3. The gate of the Caucasus is the counterpart of the gate of Gibraltar in the West.

CARLES ANDRADE 1988

Jason, the healer or redeemer, regains it in the process of his own initiation. His body becomes the Argo, a sacred vessel, supervised by gods. His soul forces, i.e., his crew members and bodyguards through whom he moves this vessel, are all heroes. He himself has to pass introductory trials in the Propontis, the forecourt of the Black Sea. After passing through the Bosporus he is already in the spiritual realm, but still guided by atavistic clairvoyance (Chiron and Phineus). When he arrives in the city of Aeëtes, he has performed all the tasks set by King Pelias, who was himself a son of Poseidon. His actual initiation, namely the capture of the Golden Fleece, is the consequence of a new set of trials, imposed by King Aeëtes, god of the wind. In his contacts with the world of the gods he wakes up from his clairvoyant state. Now he is helped by the magic force of his own consciousness, which in the myth appears as the Princess Medea, that is, "the one who thinks." Medea loves him because she loves his real spiritual being, of which she is a part.[4] This consciousness of self protects Jason against the enormous powers of his instincts. He does not have to make oxen out of the bulls in order to make them draw the plow. He is their master through the magic of his consciousness, Medea, and through the skills which he acquired through his centauric training in his youth. He can transform their ferocity into usefulness. By sowing the dragon's teeth, he brings to life what is still residing in him as fossilized aggression. The wisdom of his thinking pitches his lower instinctual forces against one another, causing them to destroy themselves. After he has overcome and reorganized his lower nature (the dragon), and after his conscious wisdom through the power of the word has directly confronted his lower nature and made it powerless in sleep, he gains access to the eternal in himself and is able to retrieve it. When he takes the shining Golden Fleece from the tree and drapes it around his shoulders to carry it aboard, he experiences the moment of his enlightenment.

The Argo was now on the way back home with King Aeëtes and his fleet in pursuit. When the enemy came too near for safety, Medea, on board the Argo, killed her half brother, the young Prince Absyrtus, and cut his body into many pieces. One after the other she threw them into the sea, forcing King Aeëtes to stop

---

4. The reader should be aware that an encounter in the course of a mythical development always has the character of a meeting of the heroine or hero with some aspect of his or her own personality.

every time he saw a part of his son's body floating upon the waters below him. He had to take each part aboard, so that eventually it would become possible to give the victim a decent burial. Still following the advice of Phineus, the Argo continued undisturbed on its journey retracing the course by which she had come. This time the Trojans could not surprise them in the narrows of the Hellespont, for Hercules, in the meantime, had defeated their city and sacked it. After they entered the Aegean Sea,[5] a strong wind from the north attacked them and blew them all the way to the island of Crete. Jason wanted to land so that he would have time for a rest and for an inspection of the keel, but a bronze giant, by the name of Talus, appeared on the top of a hill and began to hurl big rocks at them. Medea confronted the giant and bewitched him with her gaze. Soon Talus lost his steady stance. He scraped the only vulnerable spot of his body, his ankle, against a rock and all his blood streamed out of him. The Hephaestian robot now lay harmless like a toppled statue. The Argonauts could safely go ashore in Crete. After a good night's rest, the winds blew them northward. Jason navigated through the passages between the many islands in this area and steered toward Aegina. The following day saw them complete their voyage and sail all the way to Thessaly, where they arrived at their point of departure, the Bay of Pagasae.

Their arrival was a surprise. Nobody had expected them back from this dangerous expedition. The wicked King Pelias, who had had no real interest in regaining the Golden Fleece for his people, had been very pleased when the young fool Jason accepted his proposal and set out toward his doom. He was still more content when all the heroes of Greece wanted to go with Jason. Now there was nobody left who could check his wicked plans. As soon as the Argo was out to sea, Pelias began a reign of crime that began with the murder of Jason's father and mother.

The Argonauts learned about the situation and deliberated what to do. Although they were not powerful enough to take on the whole army of Iolcus, they felt their duty was to kill King Pelias.

---

5. Many adventures are told of the Argonauts on their way back, but they seem to have been either borrowed from the Odyssey, or better suited to the description of the outward voyage. Some sources steer the Argonauts up various Russian rivers via the Baltic, the Atlantic, through the Strait of Gibraltar, and into the Mediterranean Sea.

Medea stood up in their midst and suggested that she with a few of her servants should first enter the town, look around to investigate the chances for a surprise attack, and give a sign with a torch when all was clear. Jason had no objections. Looking like an old priestess, shabby, and tired, Medea succeeded in entering the city with a few of her maidens, similarly disguised. They pretended to have an important message for the king from the goddess Artemis, whose priestess she claimed to be. Led before Pelias, she told him that the goddess was pleased with him and wanted to change him into a young man, so that he would be able to beget another son to take Acastus' place. For Acastus had joined the Argonauts and was now plotting against his father. To convince the king, she showed off her powers by making herself look young and pretty and also by rejuvenating an old ram. She had the animal killed and cut into pieces, then she boiled it in a magic cauldron. Medea, the magician, uttered her incantations and in a few moments a playful little lamb had taken the place of the stocky old ram. Pelias was impressed. When Medea persuaded the three daughters of Pelias (one of whom was Alcestis) to give their father the same treatment, he had no objections to being put to sleep by means of Medea's drugs. This time, however, Medea did not chant any charms. Pelias suffered an ignominious death. While this was taking place, the servant girls had not been idle. It did not take them long to discover that the guards were not alert in the absence of the king. Soon the Argonauts, waiting in the harbor, received a torch signal from one of Medea's servants who was standing on top of the palace. They rushed into the town and took it without any resistance.

Jason finally took the Golden Fleece out of the Argo and carried it in procession to Orchomenus, the place where, years before, the ram that had carried Phrixus and Helle away, had made its appearance. He hung the Golden Fleece in the temple of Zeus. In the same town the remains of Phrixus found a proper burial. Jason then had the Argo rowed to Corinth, where it was hauled up on the beach and dedicated to Poseidon, whose sacred domain it had been able to penetrate. The rule of the stepmother had ended. Man had recaptured his spirituality.

Jason succeeds in finding his eternal spiritual being, the Golden Fleece, through the strength of Medea, his own consciousness. This enables him to overcome the dragon, his lower nature, which keeps him away from what is eternal in him. However, even as an initiate, in conscious possession of his

Golden Fleece, Jason is not yet safe from forces that attack him out of the perceptual, physical world. They function like instincts, always pursuing him. To them he has to sacrifice a part of his consciousness, viz., Medea's younger brother. This is the part of our consciousness that cannot work with totalities. We can only come to an intellectual understanding of the outer world of the senses by thinking of it as something dismembered, as if it consists of many separate entities.

A last attack from the world of Hephaestus—a motif counterbalancing the yoking of the bronze-hoofed bulls—is met head-on by Medea. The bronze giant, Talus, clumsily destroys himself when confronted by clear thinking. The first motif of the myth, the appearance and the activity of the ram, is balanced in the composition by the last deed of Medea. She sacrifices a ram and cuts it up, as she had done with Absyrtus' body. Then she brings it back to life. When our thinking directs itself to its own spiritual substance—the Golden Fleece, brought to mind by its association with the old ram—then this self-penetration will lead to a heightening of consciousness and a new, younger, and stronger ram.

———

In 431 B.C., long after the period of the mythopoetic way of thinking had faded, the Athenian playwright Euripides wrote and produced a powerful, romantic drama, Medea, in which he presented his ideas about the further development of Jason's and Medea's life, after the Golden Fleece had been found and brought home. In this play Medea is depicted as an extremely emotional and wicked witch and magician, who does not shrink even from the murder of her own children. Perhaps because that year also marked the beginning of the war with Sparta, the playwright felt the need to remind his fellow countrymen, the citizens of Athens, of their most glorious exploits fifty years earlier under Themistocles, when they had defeated the Persians, the powerful barbarians from Asia. Medea is such a barbarian in his play, an image of a typical enemy. Euripides' story, however, is not a true myth.

106

THESEUS, THE ATHENIAN

Long ago, in the great city of Athens, there lived a highly gifted man called Daedalus, a member of the royal family. He was known as a maker of wonderful mechanical things, such as self-moving dolls in all sizes, and he was also a famous architect. In his versatility and creativity, one could compare him to the later Leonardo da Vinci. To his large and well-equipped workshop came apprentices from all over the country to work with him. They all produced excellent work, otherwise they would not have been allowed to stay with the master, but none could be compared with the great Daedalus himself. Not, that is, until his own nephew started to work for him. His name was Perdix and he was the son of Daedalus' sister. At the age of twelve he began inventing tools and implements that his uncle had not yet thought of. Daedalus, who was strongly convinced of his own worth and importance, at first was astonished, but then grew angry and envious. Once, when the young boy accompanied his uncle on a walk, they climbed a high tower. In a fit of temper, Daedalus pushed young Perdix off the tower. But just as he was about to hit the ground, the goddess Athena (invisibly present) touched the screaming child, and changed him into a partridge. (Perdix means "partridge.") The boy fluttered along the ground and disappeared. For this murder, Daedalus was punished with exile from his tribe and became a man who did not belong anywhere.

However, Daedalus quite soon found another good and lucrative position in which to do his work. The ruler of the island of Crete, the well-known King Minos, wanted to be his patron. Minos, a wealthy and expansive man, ruled over ninety cities and had great fleets of merchant ships. This king was very happy to offer the great Athenian artist a position at his court, where he had him design in all its details the royal palace near the town of Cnossus, considered one of the wonders of the world. At Cnossus the royal family lived in style. A huge temple hall in the center of the building was dedicated to Zeus; adorning the walls and ledges were frescoes and sculptures of a holy symbol: the double-bladed ax, the so-called Labrys, emblem of the waning and waxing moon. From these Labryes this hall and the entire palace around were given the name labyrinth. It was to become the site of an important feat in the life of the Athenian hero Theseus.

All kings of Crete were called Minos. The first bearer of that name was a son of Zeus and the Phoenician Princess Europa, whom the father of the gods and men had abducted when she was walking along a beach on the Mediterranean Sea. One day a herd of her father's cattle was driven along the Phoenician shore. Zeus had hidden himself in the midst of the herd in the form of a majestic white bull. Princess Europa, charmed by the beauty and gentle disposition of the wonderful animal, played with him, put flowers in his mouth and strung them around his horns. She finally climbed on the bull's back and rode him triumphantly along the edge of the sea. Suddenly, the mighty animal turned toward the water, ran, and jumped into the waves with a great splash. Quickly it swam out to sea with her, far beyond the horizon, on and on, all the way to the island of Crete. Coming out of the water, the bull sank down on its knees, allowing Europa, tired and awed but not at all afraid, to climb down. Zeus then turned himself into an eagle, and in this form he impregnated Europa. Thus in due time she became the mother of a son, whom she called Minos.

Bulls play an all-important role in the Cretan, or Minoan, culture. Bulls were habitually sacrificed to Poseidon and other gods. On the occasion of sacred festivals, people loved to watch ritual performances in which graceful boys and girls somersaulted with great daring over the back of an onrushing bull. Choice white bulls of great beauty were dedicated to the god Poseidon and treated with special consideration.

Once Poseidon sent the king a snow-white bull, but made it clear that this animal was destined to be given back to him as a sacrifice. The king, however, liked this glorious bull so much that he did not have the heart to part with it. He kept it in his stable so that he could admire and enjoy it, and sacrificed a lesser bull in its stead. As could have been expected, Poseidon, a vindictive god, punished Minos severely. He caused his wife, Queen Pasiphaë, a daughter of the sun god, to fall desperately and foolishly in love with the bull. The bull returned her love, but became a great danger to the population of the island. Wild and bellowing, it ran all over destroying fields and killing people. Finally, Hercules was assigned to capture it as one of his labors. The hero took it to mainland

Greece, where it ran wild through Attica, and became known as the bull of Marathon. However, before this happened, Daedalus, who was well liked by the royal family, helped the queen in her plight by constructing a wooden cow in which she could conceal herself. Thus ensconced, she was united with the great bull and became pregnant. In due time Pasiphaë gave birth to a hybrid being, part bull, part human, called the Minotaur. This event was the cause of great embarrassment for the royal family, especially since the little Minotaur became very wild and dangerous. Again Daedalus was asked to help. He built a second labyrinth in the cellars under the palace. It consisted of a maze of passages and galleries, in the center of which the Minotaur led its hidden life. The other children of Pasiphaë were forced to live their lives with the knowledge of the monster always present in their consciousness. Especially the older Princesses Ariadne and Phaedra, and their brother, Prince Androgeus, suffered from this situation.

Minos is not really a proper name; it denotes the title held by the kings of Crete, like "pharao" in Egypt or "midas" in Phrygia. We can compare the Cretan word minos, with the Greek noun menos, which is used by Homer in the sense of "strength of mind," or "spiritual energy." The English word "mind" is of the same root, as is the German meinen, "to think," as well as Latin mens and Sanscrit manas, i.e., "mind." The word minos or its equivalent is a common title for leaders in antiquity. It appears in the form Manu in Ancient India and as Manes in Ancient Persia. We can find similar words in other language families: e.g., Menes is the name of the first Egyptian pharaoh known to history, while Manitou is the word indicating "spirit" or "supernatural power" in the language of the American Indian tribes of the Algonquin.

King Minos represents the spiritual power that gives leadership and order to Cretan culture. He is the "mind" of his people. He is archetypal man. Also the English man, German Mensch, Sanscrit manushia are from the same root as "mind."[1] Apart from what we can learn from these language comparisons, there is an indication that Minos represents archetypal man in the story of his descent. Minos is a demigod. His father, Zeus, in the form of the bull, attracted his mother, the human Princess Europa, and united himself with her in the form of an eagle. Three of the four macro-microcosmic components of the human being, man, bull, and

---

1. See: F. Hiebel, o.c.

eagle, are described as his ancestral forces. Only the lion is missing.

The myth describes how spiritual man (minos) is confronted with a powerful temptation. Out of the divine world (out of the waters of Poseidon) he is presented with the great white bull. At the same time he is ordered to give it back in sacrifice. Man, however, is not yet able to bring about this sacrifice. On the contrary, he, due to his emotional life (pictured as Queen Pasiphaë), falls in love with the beautiful bull. His giving in to the beauty of sexuality as such, instead of sacrificing it to the god of fertility, leads to the destruction of everyday life (pictured as the life of the peasants in the country), and, through the intervention of the intellect (Daedalus), makes man change himself into a new being (makes him produce a child), a wild, inharmonious hybrid. Destined to be a minos, man turns into a minotaurus; from spiritual man he becomes the mind-bull.

Daedalus, who comes to him from the outside, is the power Minos uses to realize his ideas. The power of the intellect in itself is amoral and ravenous, as depicted in the story of Perdix. Daedalus really killed the child of his sister. "Changing into a bird" is a picture of dying, after which man's soul-bird flies away. Out of calculating envy, Daedalus killed his emotional life. The fall of Perdix into the depths not only foreshadows the master's own fall after expulsion from his fatherland, but also his later punishment for the death of his son, Icarus. Pure intellect only works for its own sake. It likes to produce robots and moving puppets, nice for the royal children to play with, but not connected with the real world.

The mind-bull has to be imprisoned, otherwise Minos would not be able to continue his rule. Only through insight is man able to contain his sexual urges. Athena, goddess of practical wisdom, had taught Daedalus his craft. Now she inspires him to build a prison for the Minotaur in the form of a labyrinthine maze, deep in the palace. Concealed in the body of man, which is his palace and his prison, there is an extra prison cell, his skull, in which Daedalus, inspired by Athena (i.e., the intellect nurtured by the innate wisdom of the living body), builds the human brain, with all its convolutions, which, in the myth, is depicted as the labyrinthine maze.

Intellectual thinking, which the inhabitants of Athena's city were the first to develop, can imprison sexuality. Such thinking has a deadening, aging effect and is polar to our youthful forces of *growth and procreation. A balance has to be brought about between the two poles, otherwise human conscious life (minos) would not be possible. The attainment of clarity of consciousness demands a continual sacrifice of the growing forces of youth.*

———

Aegeus, the king of Athens, had reason to be unhappy. His two marriages had been childless, whereas his brother Pallas was the father of many sons. Pallas and his two other brothers, who ruled the rest of Attica, were always threatening to attack Aegeus and to capture his throne. He was afraid that his lack of offspring was a sign that he had offended Aphrodite, the goddess of love. Therefore he built her a shining temple in Athens and encouraged his Athenians to worship her. Then, as many other mythical kings have done, he went to Delphi to consult Apollo's oracle about begetting children. The oracle gave a positive answer, clad, however, in very obscure words. Aegeus did not want to go home before he understood what Apollo had told him. He therefore made a detour and visited his old friend Pittheus of Troezen, a small city-state in Argolis just opposite Athens at the other side of the Saronic Gulf. King Pittheus was a savant and a teacher, and it did not take him long to understand the obscure language of the oracle. According to Pittheus, the oracle had told Aegeus that it would be extremely dangerous for him to sleep with a woman before he had returned to Athens. Pittheus interpreted this to mean that in case his friend should not follow Apollo's instructions there would be born to him a son, who in due time would take the throne from his father. At that time, King Pittheus had an unmarried daughter named Aethra. He made Aegeus drink too much and arranged that he sleep in Aethra's bed. On awakening, Aegeus prevailed upon the princess should she bear a son, not to send him to Athens while he was young, as his uncles would try to kill him. Aegeus could not stay with her, as Athens needed its king. He then took his royal sword, a famous heirloom, and his sandals and hid them under a large altar stone at the side of the road. He told Aethra that when her son had grown strong enough to move the heavy stone, he should take the sandals and the sword. She then should send him to his father's palace, where he would be able to prove his identity by showing these articles. All these actions had to be completely secret, for, if Pallas should learn that Aethra was to give birth to the future king of Athens, her life, too, would be in danger.

111

Aethra indeed gave birth to a son, whom she called Theseus. Pittheus secured his daughter's safety by making it known that the god Poseidon was the father of the child she was expecting. In all probability this actually was the case. For, in the night in which she slept with Aegeus, Aethra had a dream sent by Athena, summoning her to get up and wade to an island just off shore. Here Poseidon united himself with her.[2]

Theseus grew up quietly with his mother and grandfather, and in the course of an uneventful and hidden youth, he became a noble and well-developed young man. When he was sixteen, Aethra thought that the time had come. She led him to the altar stone of which she had been thinking so often of late. There she sat down with her son and told him all she knew of his father, King Aegeus of Athens. Then she stood up and laid her hand on the altar. Theseus proved to be just strong enough to move the rock somewhat. He was elated when he was able to take the beautiful antique sword in his hands, and immediately inspected it. He was moved at the sight of his father's sandals, and found that they fitted him perfectly. This day marked the beginning of his life as a hero. Without delay he wanted to start his journey to visit his royal father in Athens. Old King Pittheus warned him of the dangers he might encounter on the way. As his uncle Pallas would not have let him pass to Athens when he heard who he was, it would have been easiest to cross the Saronic Gulf by boat, this being the fastest and safest route. His mother begged him to accept the boat that his grandfather offered him. But Theseus wanted to act just as his great hero Hercules would act, and chose instead the long and hazardous road overland.

On the way, Theseus performed six labors of justice, clearing the land of the brigands and murderers he met.

(1) His first encounter was with Periphetes, a cripple, who murdered travelers with his long, bronze club. Theseus wrestled the weapon out of his hands, and used it on the murderer himself. He kept the club, which was a good weapon, similar to the one Hercules used.

(2) On the narrow isthmus north of Corinth, the hero came upon another infamous creature, Sinis, known as "the pine-bender." When he caught a traveler, he would place him between

_____

2. There are also indications, such as "the Aegean Sea," that "Aegeus" is one of the names of Poseidon.

two young pine trees, which he had bent to the ground—he was strong enough to do so—after which he would bind the man's left foot and hand to one tree, his right hand and foot to the other. Then he would let go of the trees and tear the unfortunate victim apart. Theseus did the same to him.

(3) An enormous wild sow, a destroyer of fields and people, was his next adversary. He hunted it for a long time and finally was able to kill it. This sow was an offspring of Typhon and Echidna, the primordial monsters who also bred the Sphinx, the Nemean lion, the Hydra, and many more dangerous supersensible beasts.

(4) Close to the city of Megara, where the coast is mountainous and steep, Theseus met the strong and cruel Sciron. This bandit would sit close to the edge of the precipice and force travelers whom he had captured to wash his feet. When they bent over to do so, Sciron would kick them over the cliff, down into the waves of the Saronic Gulf. Theseus picked him up and threw him bodily into the sea.

(5) Rounding the corner of the Saronic Gulf, he entered Athenian country from the north and came upon Cercyon, a mighty wrestler, who fought with every traveler and crushed each of them to death against his massive chest. Theseus, a skillful wrestler himself, took Cercyon by the knees, and bashed his head against the ground.

(6) Not far from the holy place of Eleusis, close to Athens, he came upon the house of Procrustes, the father of Sinis, the pinebender. This old murderer was the owner of a sleeping lodge with only one bed in it. Travelers were made to fit the bed, either by stretching them when they were too short, or cutting them to size when their legs were too long. Theseus repaid him in kind.

Like Acrisius, the grandfather of Perseus, and like Laius, Oedipus' father, Aegeus, too, wanted to know from Delphi whether his development would continue toward a total renewal of his being. To each of the three kings the oracle told that this renewal would indeed take place (a son would be born), and that the old form of their royal being would be replaced by a new one. The crown prince would become king, and the son would kill his father. In the case of Aegeus this son had to be born out of wedlock, since his queen was not able to have children. Aegeus' friend wanted to help him reach this state of renovation. As in the case of Laius, it was due to the influence of Dionysus' wine that the union took place that led to the birth of this son. The entire attempt of King

113

Pittheus to make sure that it would be his daughter who would bear a child of Aegeus appears to have been inspired by the goddess Athena, who wanted a demigod on the throne of her city. She organized the coming together of Poseidon and Aethra—by means of the young woman's dream—in the same night as the princess' cohabitation with Aegeus, king of Athens, to legitimate the position of the demigod Theseus as crown prince, and later as king.

Theseus, in typical heroic fashion, grows up without any influence from either his family or his tribe. One could expect, therefore, that his development would lead to independence and consciousness of self. The first step he takes to assume this independent position consists in setting out, in a conscious, self-willed way, to connect himself with his ancestral stream. By finding the hidden ancestral sword, he changes himself into a knight without fear of reproach. By donning the sandals of his father, "he puts himself in his father's shoes," as a free deed. This clearly signifies that now he is irrevocably on his way to take over the position of his father. As an independent individual, he does not want any support from his mother's tribe or family. (He refuses the offered boat.) The journey of development which Theseus undertakes, shows him to be worthy of his name. He puts his own stamp on the journey by bringing clarity and order to the area. The name Theseus means, "one who puts things in their place."

Ordering the environment and making it safe for travelers is accomplished by Theseus by means of his own inner development. Through his labors, he first overcomes what there is in him of clumsy and crippling aggression (Periphetes). Out of this trial he gains a good weapon. Then he strengthens his powers of concentration by doing away with the tendencies that are apt to scatter his being far and wide (Sinis). Next he has to fight hard to defeat instinctive wildness (sow). Then he learns to walk along high edges of insight without losing his footing or his balance (Sciron). After this comes his combat with the crushing weight of the physical body (Cercyon). Finally, he overcomes all tendencies toward conformity, which could have destroyed his life as a heroic individual (Procrustes).

At the gate of Athens he was purified by rituals from all the blood he had spilled on the way. Then Theseus entered the town of his father and went straight to the king's palace. Aegeus did not recognize him, though he wondered who this handsome young man might be. He invited him to dine, and when meat was distributed at the table, Theseus rather demonstratively drew his beautiful sword to carve his portion. With a shock, the old king saw his own sword with its ivory hilt in the hand of the young hero and knew that his son had arrived. There was great emotion and great joy in the palace and throughout the town. The gods received sacrifices of gratitude in abundance.

When Theseus had found his position in the palace and came to know his father and what it meant to be a king, the time had come for him to show that he was Aegeus' successor, or rather his father's renewed being. He began to perform important deeds for the sake of the Athenian people, deeds too strenuous for the old king. First he overcame the revolt, which his uncle Pallas had organized against the king when he realized that the newly found crown prince threatened the succession of his own sons to the throne of Athens. In a quick campaign, Theseus, at the head of Athenian soldiers, destroyed the enemy forces. Pallas acknowledged his defeat, and had to sue for peace. Then Theseus took a really Herculean task upon himself. He went out to free his people from the dangerous bull of Marathon. This was the majestic, but bloodthirsty bull that Poseidon had given to King Minos in Crete. More than twenty years earlier, Prince Androgeus, a son of Minos, was killed by the bull when he visited Athens to participate in athletic games. In performing this deed Theseus proved himself no less strong and courageous than Hercules himself. He caught the bull and dragged it all the way up the steep acropolis, where he sacrificed it to the goddess Athena.

King Minos had been extremely unhappy at the death of his son Androgeus, whom he loved dearly. When he learned that the Minoan prince during his visit to Athens had won all the athletic contests in which he participated, the king became suspicious and soon felt convinced that his son's death had not been accidental. In revenge, the mighty sea lord of Crete imposed a cruel punishment upon the citizens of Athens. Every ninth year they were to send seven young men and seven young women to Cnossus, there to be led into the labyrinth as food for the Minotaur. In the year after Theseus' arrival the time had again come in which the tribute was to be paid to the Cretan king. The ceremonial vessel of death was ready, inspected, and equipped for the voyage. Its black sail was hung on the mast. All families with grown children anxiously awaited the day on which the lots would be cast. Theseus decided that it was his task as the crown prince to participate in the expedition and oppose the forces of evil with his heroism. King Aegeus first tried to dissuade his newly found son. But then he realized that such an attempt was really the task of the king, and that Theseus was going to perform it as the new king in his stead. Only six youths were chosen this time in addition to the seven maidens. Theseus joined them at the time of departure. King Aegeus was very moved, frightened, and proud. He had a large white sail stowed away in the boat, and made Theseus promise that he would hoist it on the way back instead of the black one of mourning, so that as soon as possible the king would know whether his son had been successful.

After sacrifices had been offered to Apollo, the black ship set sail in a southeasterly direction. The voyage did not take long. When, after two days, the ship arrived at the harbor of Cnossus, King Minos himself came down to look at the Athenians and to count them. He had heard many rumors about Prince Theseus, and was intrigued to see him on his island at the head of the Athenian victims.

An altercation took place between the old and the young king, in the course of which Minos challenged Theseus' alleged descent from Poseidon. He took a golden ring from his finger and threw it into the sea[3] with a contemptuous gesture. Then he asked Theseus to retrieve it with Poseidon's help, if he could. When Theseus asked, in turn, that Minos should prove his own descent from Zeus, the king spoke in prayer, "O Father Zeus, hear me!" Immediately, lightening flashed in the bright afternoon and thunder clapped ominously. Without a word, Theseus dived into the sea and emerged shortly afterwards, not only with the ring, but also holding a golden wedding diadem. At the moment his son hit the water, Poseidon sent the water nymphs in all directions to find the treasures for him. This deed made the name of Theseus famous throughout Crete. When, escorted by Cretan soldiers, the group of victims marched to the labyrinth with Theseus in the lead, many citizens of Cnossus cast an admiring eye on the radiant prince, who was the son of a god.

Most profoundly moved by his appearance and behavior was

---

3. The myth of the discarded ring retrieved by water beings is very common in tales, e.g., in Grimm's fairy tale "The White Snake," where it occurs twice, and in the Dutch folk legend "The Lady of Stavoren."

Ariadne, a daughter of King Minos. She did not want him to be destroyed by her unfortunate, but ferocious half brother, the Minotaur. Immediately, she summoned Daedalus, the master builder, and demanded from him the solution to the riddle of the labyrinth. Daedalus gave her the solution in a practical form: a magic ball of thread. The loose end was to be tied to the post of the entrance door and the ball placed on the floor, where it would start rolling in pursuit of the Minotaur. Automatically it would unwind its twisted path, around corners and through straight sections, to the place where the monster would be.

Secretly, in the dark of the night, Ariadne sent a message to Theseus, promising that she would help him kill the hated Minotaur, if he would swear to take her back with him to Athens as his wife. Theseus readily swore that he would do so. Then Ariadne gave him the magic ball and told him what to do. Theseus thanked her with all his heart, and without waiting for daylight to come went into the labyrinth, where at the end of the ball of yarn he found the Minotaur in deep sleep. In one bound the hero jumped on top of the monster, and in an uncanny and ferocious fight in the dark, killed it with his bare hands. He then picked up the thread and followed it back to the entrance, rolling it up as he walked. There he found Ariadne waiting for him with a kiss. It was still dark when the two of them led the group of Athenians back to the harbor where the captain of their ship waited impatiently. The moment they were aboard, he hoisted the black sail and sped away in the dark night. Aboard the ship Theseus gave Ariadne, as a wedding present, the sparkling diadem he had retrieved from the domain of Poseidon. All the young people aboard the ship of death were happy to celebrate their deliverance from the cruel Minotaur, and started making preparations for Theseus' wedding.

Of his first six heroic deeds performed on the way to Athens, only the slaying of the wild sow depicts the uprooting of a true instinct. The other five deeds depict the elimination of habits of which the hero was conscious. These appear in the image of bandits, i.e., humans. Proof of his right to succeed his father is his ownership of the ancestral sword. Immediately he starts using this sword to fight the enemy of his fatherland, the tribe of Pallas and his fifty sons. Theseus, the individual, overcomes the tribal forces. His capture and sacrifice of the bull of Marathon finally fulfilled the demand which Poseidon had put to Minos. Again Theseus overcomes a powerful instinct in himself while, at the same time,

119

healing the wounds of his people. The Minotaur, the offspring of the great bull that had been running wild in their country, was still there as a source of anguish and sorrow. To complete his work as the redeemer, Theseus also has to overcome the mind-bull within himself. Regularly, the strength of youth has to be sacrificed to restrain sexuality in the confinement of Daedalus' labyrinth. When Theseus takes the expedition in hand, the youthful forces have someone to organize them and act as their representative.

Just after their arrival in Crete, a confrontation takes place between Minos, in the world of Zeus, with thunder and lightening, and Theseus in the world of Poseidon, surrounded by water nymphs. Without realizing it, Minos throws his daughter's wedding ring into the sea. Theseus retrieves it, together with another ornament given him by a sea goddess. After having become acquainted with the world of Aegeus, his mortal father, the hero has to immerse himself in the kingdom of his real, i.e., his spiritual father, Poseidon, who helps him from afar without any personal involvement. At the threshold of his beginning initiation, the hero proves that he represents the god Poseidon, whose kingdom surrounds Crete, and shows that he had expiated the cause of the water god's anger by finally sacrificing the wild bull to the gods. Apparently Poseidon does not take offense that this sacrifice had not been made to him at Cnossus but on the acropolis to the goddess Athena.[4]

In the tense atmosphere of the victims' march toward the place of execution, Ariadne, whose name means "the purest one," is stricken with love for Theseus, just as Medea had been as soon as she saw Jason. As the daughter of Minos, Ariadne is "mind's (Minos') purest thought." Daedalus' creative force gives Ariadne a clue (a clew of yarn), which, as an individual probe, enters the instrument of intellectual thinking (the brain, the labyrinth), and has to be followed back out of it. Pure thinking (Ariadne), with the help of creative thinking (Daedalus), gives to the human self (Theseus, the organizer) the direction to overcome the mind-bull in himself, i.e., his aggressive, egotistic, brain-bound-labyrinthine thinking. Theseus' spiritual being, and his pure spiritual thinking

---

4. In the substitution of these two Olympian gods one can see a faintly ominous indication of the future decline of the Minoan thalossocracy, which would be taken over much later by the Athenian sea power in the Delian League.

(Ariadne) confront and recognize each other. They discover their relationship, and intend to become one in marriage. Theseus already has the wedding gifts with him, the golden ring, unwittingly given by her father Minos, and the diadem provided by his father Poseidon.

The marriage of Theseus and Ariadne took place on the island of Naxos at the halfway point of the voyage to Athens. In the night, however, Theseus received a message in a dream. The god Dionysus, on his way back from India with his retinue of satyrs and maenads, appeared to him and demanded Ariadne for himself. In great awe and haste, Theseus left the island and abandoned his bride. She cried when she woke up to find that she was alone on the shores of Naxos. But already the ships of Dionysus were rapidly approaching. The god married Ariadne without delay, and in the course of the years to come they would have many children. At the end of her earthly life, he would take her with him to Olympus, and put her wedding diadem in the sky as a constellation, known as the Northern Crown. After leaving Naxos, Theseus interrupted his voyage once more, at the island of Delos, birthplace of the god Apollo, where he offered sacrifices to the god. The last part of the voyage was hard sailing. Strange winds out of contrary directions tried to keep him from reaching Attica. When the helmsman finally succeeded in approaching the coast, Theseus had become so engrossed in sailing, that he forgot to change the black sail for the shining white one. Meanwhile, Aegeus, anxiously expecting his return, watched from high rocks where he could see far to the south. When the moment arrived for which he had been waiting, it was not the joyful signal of the new white sail that met his eyes, but the somber black of mourning. Convinced that the mission had failed and that Theseus had been devoured by the Minotaur, he decided to destroy himself, that is, his old self, and jumped to his death in the sea (since then called the Aegean Sea).

At the same time, another drowning took place in another part of the same sea not far from Crete, when young Icarus fell to his death. Daedalus and his son, Icarus, had been imprisoned by King Minos inside the labyrinth when the king found out that it was the master builder who had given away the secret of the maze to Princess Ariadne. There was no possibility for Daedalus to escape from this prison, neither by land nor by sea. Therefore, he chose the only way open, a flight through the air. Out of feathers and wax he fabricated sets of wings in two sizes, and studying and imitating the birds, he and his son learned to fly. To overcome their heaviness and escape their prison was a great joy for both father and son, especially for young Icarus, who took to flying quite naturally. In spite of his father's warnings, the enthusiastic boy flew much too high and came too close to the sun. The wax melted, he lost his wings, and plunged to his death in the sea, Daedalus, though overcome by sorrow, succeeded in flying on, far to the west, to the Italian island of Sicily, where he lived until the end of his life.

The abandonment of Ariadne by Theseus is a riddle for which diverse explanations have been put forward. The most reasonable of these, we think, is that Ariadne, the pure daughter of mind, is Theseus' spiritualized thinking, his individual consciousness. For a short moment he is able to experience her as his own, after overcoming his egotistic thinking in the labyrinth. But he has to care for more than his individual development. Being a king, he would be married to his people, and would to a great extent be absorbed in tribal life, and have to postpone his individual development. When he abandons Ariadne, she is taken up in the spiritual realm of the gods, to become a goddess herself, and the wife of the god Dionysus. When Theseus' ship is within sight of his home, fate makes him forget to change the sails, and his father makes a place for him on the throne of Athens by, of his own free will, departing from life. At the same time, Daedalus, his uncle, also goes away by flying to another part of the world.[5] Theseus now has to go forward alone. By killing the mind-bull he had purified his creative intellect, old Daedalus, so that it, turning upon itself—imprisoned—could learn to transcend matter and take flight.[6] However, the first attempt at pure, non-Minotauric thinking is still childishly immature and vulnerable. Its child has to die from lack of restraint. Only the serious Daedalus can go to the culture of the West. Minos pursues him there and is himself killed. In this manner, the third power of the past (Minos) also steps out of Theseus' life.

---

5. As a counterpoint in the composition of Daedalus' story, the death of young Icarus at the end balances the murder of young Perdix at the beginning.

6. The image of wings attached to a man should be seen with the poetic eye of mythologic perception, not with the literal eye of the technician. Daedalus' flight across the sea disclosed trust in his intellect and represented an "imagination of thinking." (F. Hiebel, *The Gospel of Hellas,* p. 50)

At this time Theseus was free to enter the mature phase of his life and to become king of the Athenians in his own right. He was an enlightened king, who succeeded in uniting the twelve parts of Attica into a federal arrangement. His people liked the democratic attitude of their young king although, like his enemies, they were well aware of his strength. He knew how to organize his own life in conjunction with the life of his tribe. His influence reached out beyond the borders of Attica. King Theseus became known as a champion of humanity who was able to help and comfort other heroes in need. Oedipus, banished from Thebes in his old age, found in Theseus understanding, and in Attica a place to rest and die. Hercules, crazed after murdering his own wife and children, found comfort and was brought back to his senses. On a later occasion it was Theseus who initiated Hercules into the Eleusinian Mysteries.

The short time in which Theseus, after killing the Minotaur, is united with his spiritual counterpart Ariadne, gives him the strength to perform his duties as king in an enlightened and organized way. In his private development, however, the enigmatic abandonment of Ariadne is the cause of great uncertainty and turmoil.

From then on he often appeared in the company of his wild and boisterous friend Pirithoüs, the Lapith, who acted as his alter ego. Together they hunted the Caledonian boar, and went on an expedition against the Amazons, taking their queen, Antiope, back with them to Athens, though not against her will. As a result, invasions and great battles with Amazons took place on Greek soil. Antiope, also called Hippolyte, became the mother of Theseus' son Hippolytus. When Pirithoüs wanted to marry Hippodamia, he invited all his friends and relations, as well as the gods, to the wedding. His cousins, the centaurs, were there too. Not used to drinking wine, they drank it undiluted and got out of hand. Becoming more and more wild, they dragged the bride away, and attacked the other guests. The wedding degenerated into an enormous battle, in which Theseus was everywhere, fighting with all his might. Finally, the centaurs were chased away. But they always remained an unruly element in the country.

Theseus then decided to marry and took as his bride the Cretan Princess Phaedra, Ariadne's sister. The connection with Crete was beneficial for Athens and it was a successful marriage. When children were born to them, Theseus sent his illegitimate son,

Hippolytus, to Troezen where he was adopted by old King Pittheus. In Eleusis, Phaedra by chance met this son of her husband and fell desperately in love with him. But Hippolytus, the son of an Amazon, was not interested in women, and most definitely not in his father's second wife. In despair, Phaedra hanged herself, after accusing Hippolytus, in a letter to Theseus, of attacking her. Theseus did not believe in his son's innocence and cursing him, sent him away. While Hippolytus was driving his chariot along the coastal road, Aphrodite, looking with displeasure on any man who held no love for women, sent a sea monster after him. Riding a huge wave, it frightened his horses, and Hippolytus was thrown from his chariot and killed.

Both Theseus and Pirithoüs having lost their wives, advanced on Argos with an army and kidnapped the most beautiful woman in the world, the famous Helen, a daughter of Zeus, and still a child at the time. They took her to a friend's house in Attica, where Theseus' mother, Aethra, looked after her until she would be old enough to marry. Then Pirithoüs wanted to kidnap a daughter of Zeus as well. Outrageous as was his nature, he wanted to marry the noblest of them all, none less than Persephone, queen of the netherworld.

Theseus and Pirithoüs went to the underworld and succeeded in penetrating the gates of Hades' palace. The lord of the dead, appearing to be friendly, invited them to sit down and wait a while on a bench. Nevermore could they move out of this chair of forgetfulness. During four long years they had to sit there in frustration and pain. Finally, Hercules, after freeing Prometheus from the Caucasian rock, came down to Hades to fulfill his task of capturing Cerberus. He was astonished to see his former benefactor sitting there, together with his friend. With his mighty arms he wrenched Theseus loose from the stone seat, though not without maiming him. But of Pirithoüs, who was not a demigod, Persephone would not let go.

Many things happened during the four years that Theseus was detained in Hades. The Argonauts had sailed to fetch the Golden Fleece; Castor and Pollux, the brothers of Helen, had come from Sparta with an army to raze several towns in Attica and put a prince—whose father had been banished by the old King Aegeus—upon the throne in Athens. Then they took their young sister back home with them.

When Theseus returned to the physical world, he had lost much of his strength, and did not feel able to recapture the throne. He left his country to live in Crete, but a storm blew his ship off course, causing him to land on the tiny island of Skyros. Here, Theseus, walking about with the local king, was treacherously pushed off a high cliff, and died the way his father, as well as Perdix and Icarus, had died.

Theseus, a figure of strength and authority, as well as a source of human understanding and love, is often disturbed and unhappy because he remembers the purest and most spiritual moments of his life at the time he was married to Ariadne, whom he had to give up to Dionysus. His aggressive tendencies, which he had been able to overcome as a young man on his first journey to Athens, raise themselves again, and are acted upon by his alter, or rather, his lower ego, Pirithoüs, "the versatile one." The expedition to the nation of the Amazons, and its violent backlash, is the first result of the cooperation between Theseus and Pirithoüs. The result is the birth of Hippolytus, "unshackled horse." Pirithoüs attempts to counterbalance the wildness of the Amazons by marrying Hippodamia, "the lady horse tamer." However, the instincts within him, his centaurs, do not want to be tamed by her. Both lower and higher self, Pirithoüs and Theseus, fight them heroically, but they cannot overcome them completely.

Theseus, wanting to recapture as much as possible of his own spiritual self, marries Ariadne's sister, Phaedra, whose name means "shining one." Some years of quiet growth are now his share. Then the unintentional return to the scene of the Hippolytus force violently disturbs this development. Phaedra is overcome by this "unshackled horse," and they both perish.

Theseus' next attempt to recapture his lost spiritual self is when he kidnaps young Helen, a demigoddess, whose being, just like Ariadne's, belongs to the world of the stars. The name Helen means "moon." Through her, he again wants to come back to Ariadne, but this time on a higher level.

Since this attempt, although successful, is premature, the Pirithoüs in him wants to repeat the experience on a still higher level and kidnap a real goddess. He choses Persephone, the queen of the world of the spirits. Going down to Hades before death and without a long and serious preparatory training, amounts to a forced initiation. This can only end in disaster. Theseus becames insane. No longer can he rule the country, and his enemies help another king to the throne. For years, the inner life of Theseus stagnates in darkness, fear, and forgetfulness. His rescue comes as a result of the deeds of love he had performed in his life. Hercules wrenches him out of the darkness, makes him abandon Pirithoüs, and restores his sanity. But when Theseus comes back to the world, he had lost his powers.

The last years and the end of his life are insignificant.

THE *ILIAD*

War broke out in 1200 B.C. between a federation of small Mycenaean kingdoms from the Greek mainland and the mighty kingdom of Troy, also called Ilion, on the Northwest Coast of Asia Minor. Both peoples were of the same race, but their ways of life had developed in different directions. The Mycenaean lords were already showing the individualism that their successors, the Greeks, would exercise in their private lives. The Trojans, on the other hand, had a typical Asiatic tribal culture. Their old and venerable king, Priam, had fifty sons and twelve daughters, who lived together with families of their own in the great palace of Troy.

One of these sons, Prince Paris, had once abducted Helen, the queen of Mycenaean Sparta. Considered the most beautiful woman in the world, she represented the essence of Hellas. Every Greek hero wanted to marry her. When she chose Menelaus, the blond king of Sparta, the others swore to defend her under all circumstances. So it came about that the abduction of the queen of a small country led to an all-out war between the East and the West that lasted ten long years.

The latter part of this war is described in a lengthy epic poem, called the *Iliad*. It was composed and compiled by an uncommonly gifted poet, known as Homer, a clairvoyant storyteller. (Tradition tells us that he was blind like Tiresias and perceived only with the inner eye.) The central theme of the *Iliad* is the terrible anger of one of the Mycenaean captains, the demigod Achilles, son of King Peleus, one of the Argonauts, and the sea goddess Thetis. Achilles' enormous anger assumes the dimension of a phenomenon of nature, such as a thunderstorm. The source of his anger is threefold: from a quarrel with his commander in chief, King Agamemnon of Argos, about his concubine, a captured Trojan girl, whom Agamemnon had taken away from him; from his wrath over the death of his friend Patroclus, who had put on Achilles' armor when the latter had withdrawn from fighting, and so had been killed by Hector; from the fury that arose in his fight against the great Trojan hero Hector, who had killed his friend.

129

Achilles is a demigod who frequently is in contact with the gods, with his mother, Thetis, and with Athena, who likes him. His consciousness rises and falls with his emotions. Lacking compassion, reverence, or conscience, his "baneful rages" give him the strongest feeling of self. But, at the end, he finally overcomes his anger and shows a germinal love in a meeting with old King Priam, who had the courage to come to his tent in the Mycenaean camp to ransom the body of his son, Prince Hector.

The Olympian gods take an eager interest in the war: some support the Greeks; others are on the side of the Trojans. Besides Achilles and Hector, Homer introduces a great many heroes on both sides. The fact that the enemy is treated in a positive way throughout the poem indicates that Homer wanted to present something other than a patriotic narration of an episode in the great war. The fight between Achilles and Hector represents the struggle between two cultures, two ages, two stages of consciousness. Achilles, the Mycenaean, fights for himself alone, not really caring about the Mycenaeans. Hector, the Trojan, fights as a member of the royal clan for the power of his house. Achilles, as a representative of a new, Western world, introduces the awakening personality. The development of clear thinking, in which the shrewd hero Odysseus excels, brings the war to its end. Hector is the last representative of an Oriental, dreamlike collectivity ruled by priestly royal families. Achilles, Hector, and Odysseus are the main characters in Homer's composition. The death of Hector brings about the end of tribal, nonindividualistic, group consciousness. The triumph of Achilles shows how human individuality begins its development. The cunning of Odysseus introduces the new power of the intellect, which it was the mission of Greek culture to develop.

THE *ODYSSEY*

The Hero

With the *Iliad*, Homer composed a wonderful introduction to his other epic poem, the *Odyssey*. In contrast to the *Iliad*, which is an epic tableau dealing with whole armies of men, the *Odyssey* is a grandiose myth and has only one hero, Odysseus, after whom it was named. Both epics, each on its own level, have exercised great influence on Greek feeling, thinking, and culture. Their study, recitation, and discussion formed the basis for Greek moral and artistic education. Roman poets later imitated the epics, and classical scholarship kept them in the focus of its attention from the time of the Renaissance until the present.

In the *Odyssey*, Homer used the vehicle of a homecoming story with a basis in historical fact for his superb mythopoetic thinking. A great hero comes back from the war on a voyage taking as long as the war itself, and has many adventures along the way.

In the introduction to the *Odyssey*, the Proem, the poet describes his hero as a resourceful person, a man of many devices. He has seen more of the world, known and unknown, than his fellow Mycenaean leaders, who only know their way within their own city-states and on the battlefield at Troy. He visited many countries and learned to understand the ways in which people lived in diverse places. He went through great and prolonged suffering "trying to save his life and to secure the homecoming of his men" for whom he greatly cared. However, because of their shortcomings they died. What happened to his crewmen constitutes an elaborate depiction of their master's personal development. He proved himself to be a shrewed and creative thinker, showing great curiosity and interest in the world. He put an end to the devastating war against the Trojans by inventing a hollow wooden horse. Disguised as a beggar, he had the courage to reconnoiter within the very walls of Troy. Helen, the abducted queen of Sparta, for whose sake the war was being fought, recognized him and secretly spoke with him, amazed and full of admiration. Later, on his return home, he defeated the powerful Cyclops by means of a daring plan, escaped the cannibalistic Laestrygones by exercising caution, and, at the end of his journey, killed his wife's suitors after careful preparation and by skillfully using a sudden opportunity. On the way, he steered through Scylla and Charybdis, and was alert enough to overcome the deadly powers of the Sirens and the great attractions of Circe, Calypso, and Nausicaä. The father god, Zeus, called Odysseus "the wisest man alive," and Athena, the goddess of thinking, was his constant protector and friend. Old Nestor too, the prototype of human wisdom, said of him: "During the war there was not a man that dared to match his wits with the admirable Odysseus." But he was not only resourceful and wise, he was also humble enough to endure the most outrageous humiliations when he eventually arrived in his kingdom.

On his voyage home, he had to perform fourteen major trials through which, like Hercules, Theseus, and many other heroes before him, he advanced on the path of inner development. The most important of these trials or "labors" was his visit to the world of the dead, that is, his staying among spiritual beings.

The *Odyssey* is a dramatic story based on pictorial thinking. The mythical adventures it depicts have ramifications on many levels, including those that are social, psychological, religious, and historical.[1] In this study we try to approach that level on which the trials of Odysseus, the archetype of a Greek hero, appear as stations along his way of initiation.

When, long ago, Odysseus was visited by King Agamemnon and King Menelaus, and summoned to do his share in the war against the Trojans, he was still the young king of the nation of Ithaca, a small rocky island off the West Coast of Greece. He was married to Penelope who, like he, "had received from Athena matchless gifts: a great skill in fine handicrafts, an excellent brain, and a genius for getting her own way." They had an infant son, Telemachus.

---

1. John H. Finley in his *Odyssey*, pp. 56-57, distinguishes four classes in Odysseus' adventures. "First there are those involving his companions' errors. . . Secondly some adventures chiefly concern natural wonders and perils. Third . . . the Cyclopes and Phaeacians show societies below and above the known societies of Greece. The fourth class . . . is of an inward character: it concerns states of mind." Contrary to Finley, in this author's reading, all four classes concern states of soul and mind.

Through the pictorial language of mythopoetic thinking, the hero is here presented at an advanced stage of his inner development. He has already reached maturity and has found his spiritual identity in his wife, Penelope, and lived his life in spiritual union with her. He also succeeded in renewing himself in the form of his son, who during his absence grows up in the loving care of Penelope. At the right moment, he will take over his father's scepter and position.

Although Telemachus grows up without his father's presence in the royal palace of Ithaca, many are present to tell him about his absent father and contribute to his education, so that the ideals of Odysseus are living within him. People are always reminded of his father when they meet Telemachus. In addition to his mother, there are his grandparents Laertes and Anticleia, and such friends of the family as Phemius the minstrel, Halitherses the seer, and Mentor the counselor, as well as the faithful servants Eumaeus, the swineherd, and Eurycleia, his father's old nurse, the prudent keeper of the household. Still, Telemachus longs for his father. When the news finally arrives in Ithaca that the war is over and won, both he and his mother are filled with eager expectations. They know that the heroes are on their way home. But as the years pass and Odysseus does not return, it becomes more and more difficult for the young prince to keep his convictions alive. When, after three or four more years, a group of young noblemen start living in the palace and putting pressure on his mother to marry one of them and to admit to herself that her husband cannot be alive anymore, the adolescent Telemachus becomes full of confusion and suffering.

Some time before the suitors arrive in Odysseus' palace to harass his wife and his young son, the hero himself, after losing all his men and ships in the course of his trials, arrives alone on the faraway island of Ogygia. Here he stays for seven years, loved by the graceful nymph Calypso, a daughter of Atlas. Once rested from the exhaustion of his travels, Odysseus is filled with longing to continue his voyage home.

At the end of his stay with Calypso, Odysseus' absence has lasted twenty years and Telemachus is twenty years of age. In Ithaca the situation for Odysseus' wife and son has become unbearable. The suitors are ruining Odysseus' possessions, eating his supplies, and depleting his herds. Telemachus is depressed, as is Odysseus in faraway Ogygia.

At Athena's initiative, the gods act to end this stalemate. She speaks to her father, Zeus, and asks him to send his messenger Hermes, the winged god, to force Calypso to release Odysseus. She herself wants to go to Ithaca to "instill a little more spirit into Odysseus' son." Together the two divine beings set out from Olympus. Hermes, the god of action, skimming over the waves, arrives in far Ogygia and gives the nymph Zeus' command. Athena, the goddess of wisdom, visits Telemachus, in the form of Mentes, a friend of the family, and assures him that his father is alive and most likely on his way home. She tells the young prince that he looks remarkably like his father, and makes him take his father's place at the table and speak up to the suitors. Then, disguised as the counselor Mentor, she goes with him by boat at night to the continent to gather information about his father among the chieftains who had returned from Troy. Thus Telemachus begins a short odyssey of his own.

When the war is over, Odysseus departs from Troy with what is left of his soldiers in twelve ships, each with a crew of fifty men. As their king and commander, he is the one who makes the decisions. The men put these into effect without completely wanting to know what they were doing or why. They work for Odysseus and represent the forces of his will. The ships are their vehicles and dwellings when they are on the water. As is the case with all dwelling places in mythopoetic thinking, the ships depict the physical body, of which Odysseus is in charge.

It is shown in the epic that without Odysseus' presence his men cannot function properly. Those who travel alone to the lotus-eaters do not come back. But for his presence, the Cyclops would have eaten them all, and Circe would have kept them as swine. They would have suffered shipwreck on the shore of the Sirens and fallen prey to either Scylla or Charybdis. On the two occasions when Odysseus fell asleep, first coming back from Aeolus with all the contrary winds in a bag, and later on the island Trinacria surrounded by Helios' sacred cows, they act without showing any sign of responsibility. Eventually, they all perish.

In the course of the first four adventures, Odysseus loses eleven of his twelve ships and crews, retaining only the ship he lives on and the men directly under his command. With these he confronts the Cyclops, stays for a year with Circe, visits the netherworld, and survives the Sirens. Six of his men are eaten by Scylla; the rest he loses in the wreck they suffer as a punishment for stealing and eating the cattle of the sun god. On the Atlantean islands of Ogygia and Scheria, Odysseus is utterly alone.

In the course of his odyssey, the hero gradually loses his crew and his ships. Every force in him which is not filled with his consciousness disappears through his trials; until the core of his being, Odysseus himself, stays alone with the nymph Calypso for seven years. She loves him and teaches him all the secrets of the past.

The physical body is here depicted as twelve ships, each inhabited and moved by fifty crew members, images of the forces of will at work in the organs and muscles. The activities of such forces are outside our consciousness, just as the crew members do their work without individual responsibility. When Odysseus' development has made it possible for him to lead a spiritual life without recourse to the body, then he may rest for seven years to assimilate his experiences and renew his being.

The *Odyssey*, Part I

As Telemachus learned during his visit with old Nestor, Odysseus' departure from Troy ten years earlier had been hasty. His ships quickly arrived at the island of Tenedos opposite Troy, but he returned to the abandoned battlefield to assist his commander in chief, Agamemnon, by performing the final sacrifices to the goddess Athena. Because she was the goddess of cities and also worshiped by the Trojans, religious rituals were to be performed in her honor which would put the seal on Troy's destruction. On the other hand, she had been a strong and loyal supporter of Agamemnon's army and had led it to victory by making use of the sagacity of Odysseus. In contrast to Ares, who lives in brute and violent fighting, Athena inspires prudent generalship. Later, Athena will show her appreciation for the sacrifices by granting Agamemnon and those who had assisted him a voyage home without problems. Odysseus she rewarded by becoming his friend and supporter. After the rituals were performed, he immediately set sail again. The wind which helped him leave the Trojan shore, this time blew his ships in the wrong direction, that is, to the north.

Odysseus and his men landed north of Troy and, as if the war was still on, they raided the city of the Ciconians, a tribe of Thracians who had been allies of the Trojans. He took the town by storm and his soldiers, breathing vengeance and still full of anger, murdered whomever they met and looted whatever took their fancy. Only the local priest of Apollo, his family and his house, was spared by Odysseus. As a recompense, Odysseus received many leather sacks of a special sweet, strong wine, which he saved for later use. The soldiers all became drunk on the looted wine and held a feast on the beach. In a sudden counterattack, mounted Ciconians from the countryside charged down upon them, and killed more than seventy of Odysseus' soldiers in a battle that continued through the night. Odysseus lost six men from each ship.

After an irresolute and hesitant beginning, Odysseus loses the wildest of his men in a nighttime battle. This trial brings an initial and primitive purge. Odysseus loses the least cultivated forces that live in all parts of his soul in a slight, but nevertheless balanced purification. Each ship loses the same number of "trouble-makers."

Then, a fierce north wind sent them on their way. For two days and two nights they had to stay awake and tend their stations. The sea was covered with dark clouds and there was no visibility. In great distress, they had to help the helmsmen by holding their oars straight down like leeboards. Odysseus' total being was being aligned and directed by the task of steering and guiding the ship. At the crucial moment they were not able to round Cape Malea to head west and then north to Ithaca. For nine long days and nights, the ships were blown south instead, all the way to the other end of the sea, where they rested on the beach.

Three explorers were sent out, but they did not return. Odysseus himself went after them with a few men, all armed. They found their friends lying down under trees, gazing ahead open-eyed and dreaming. They had eaten the sweet-smelling fruit of the lotus plant, given them by friendly natives. They were not aware of their environment, had forgotten all about the war, and did not know where they were going. Against their will, Odysseus had his explorers rescued. They were tied and marched to the ship where they were kept in shackles until the effects of the drug had worn off.

Still at the beginning of his voyage, Odysseus has to be quick and strong enough to pass this difficult trial. Exhausted from maintaining his concentration during the stormy beginning of his soul voyage, he has to resist the strong temptation to collapse in fatigue and cease trying to maintain his consciousness of self. If he had not forcibly broken off the exploratory contacts which unwittingly he was already making, he would never have reached

*home and Greek civilization would have been denied his leader-
ship.*

At this moment in his odyssey the hero had to pass a very severe
test. He came with his men to the land of the Cyclops during a
foggy, moonless night. Guided by "some god," the twelve ships ran
ashore. Next morning, after a very deep sleep, the men found
themselves in a fine harbor of a beautiful island. The shore of the
mainland was not far away and they could see many wild goats
running about. Eleven crews remained behind to rest with their
ships and to hunt on the uninhabited island, while Odysseus had
his own ship rowed across to the mainland. He selected his twelve
best men to go with him to explore inland. Odysseus felt a
foreboding that they were on their way to meet an "inhuman"
force. Before long they came to a large cave in the side of a
mountain, where a giant had made his home. They entered with
caution. In the evening, when the owner, the one-eyed Cyclops
Polyphemus, drove his flocks of goats and sheep into the cave, he
was at first not aware of his visitors, who had been eating goat meat
and drinking milk. When they saw whose property they had been
consuming, they became deadly pale and wanted to flee. But they
were trapped. On entering, Polyphemus had closed his cave with a
huge, round stone. Never would they have been able to roll it away.
Full of apprehension, they could only wait. While milking his goats,
the giant noticed the thirteen little people, took two of them by the
feet and in an unconcerned way dashed their brains out and
devoured their bodies. None of the Greeks could sleep that night.
The next morning the Cyclops ate two more of the men, and again
two more when he came back at night with his flocks. By now the
cunning Odysseus had formed a plan. During the day he made a
weapon out of a stake of olive wood, which he found lying against
the wall, by sharpening it and hardening it in the fire. At night, after
Polyphemus had devoured two more of his men, Odysseus
addressed him, offering him a beaker of the excellent wine that he
had brought with him. This was the wine the priest of Apollo had
given him when Odysseus spared his life during the battle with the
Ciconians. The giant drank it greedily and asked for more. He
showed his appreciation by asking Odysseus' name. "My name is
Outis," Odysseus said. (It sounds like a friendly abbreviation of his
name, but it means "nobody.") "Well, friend Outis," said the
monster, "I will eat you last." As soon as he had fallen into a deep,
drunken sleep, Odysseus and his six comrades burned out the

Cyclops' solitary eye. The other Cyclopes heard him screaming, but when, in answer to their questions, he cried out that "nobody" was hurting him, they paid no further attention. In the morning the blinded giant sat down at the entrance of his cave to make sure that no one would be able to escape among the animals on their way to pasture. Odysseus, however, had rounded up eighteen of the rams and roped them together, three by three. Under the middle one of each group hung one of his men, unnoticed by Polyphemus. Odysseus himself escaped by hanging under the neck and stomach of the biggest ram in the flock, holding on to its fleece with fingers and toes. They boarded their ship and rowed away as fast as they could. The giant threw some huge rocks and twice nearly hit their ship. Greatly shocked by the terrible death of their companions, the men in the twelve ships hastened on their way.

The episode on the island of the Cyclopes depicts a physical birth as the picture of a spiritual birth. Guided by "some god," i.e., by his guardian angel, man's spiritual being approaches the earthly form, as if coming upon an as yet uncultivated island with great possibilities. The wild goats, full of curiosity and running around nibbling at everything,[2] are images of innate tendencies and dispositions. Odysseus, the incarnating self, with his twelve companions, the senses,[3] enters the cave, i.e., the body, in which the chemical processes connected with the production and digestion of milk are everywhere noticeable. This body, if he is not alert, is going to be his spiritual death or his entombment. The senses, his companions, want to steal what they like, and then run—the typical behavior of senses. But Odysseus himself stays to meet the being of his body and exchange the gifts of hospitality, so that he might learn from the experience. The hero then finds himself imprisoned in the cave of his body, where the untamed forces of nature (the brutal Cyclops Polyphemus) hold sway. Some of Odysseus' friends are eaten by the monster. Those are the senses most deeply connected with the physical world, such as taste, smell, and touch. They are absorbed (swallowed) by the gigantic unconscious forces of the instincts. This would have happened to all of them, even to Odysseus himself, if he had not

---

2. One finds a similar description in Grimm's fairy tale "The Wolf and the Seven Little Goats."

3. There are many more than six senses. Steiner distinguishes twelve senses, not all of which use a separate organ of the physical body.

invented a solution. To overcome this wildness with the sharp sword of his thinking, usually the best weapon in the battle with instincts, would not have been possible in this case. He would never have been able to leave his prison again, for Polyphemus closed it at night with an enormous tombstone. The monster, therefore, had to be defeated, but not killed. With the help of the product of Dionysus' strong undiluted wine, Polyphemus is made to lose his wits. Then a purification takes place through fire, under the guidance and with the help of Athena's wisdom, for the olive tree is sacred to the goddess Athena. The poem relates that Odysseus finds a stake of olive wood, which he sharpens and hardens in the fire. However, this cannot be taken literally. Olive trees, as every Greek knew, do not produce straight stakes of any length, and putting one in the fire will only scorch it.

This is the first instance of Athena's continuous care for Odysseus. At this early stage of his development he is not yet able to have personal contact with her.

Through his own cunning, Odysseus escaped being devoured by the world of matter, and this gave his development a strong impulse. He and his men then arrived at a paradisiac island, surrounded by a bronze wall and floating on water. It is the realm of Aeolus, the warden of gales and seasons, and his six sons and six daughters, married to each other, without offspring, who rule the months of the year. The Greeks are invited to stay, and for a whole month they rest, feast, and tell about their adventures. Odysseus is now far removed from the physical world and has drifted into a region where motion and direction are given to the travelers on the paths of life by a king who marshals the winds of fate. Aeolus, in friendship, wants to give Odysseus a shortcut to his destination by leaving the favorable west wind free to blow. He presents him with all the other winds imprisoned in an enormous bag, which he may take with him and carefully watch. For nine days Odysseus is able to stay alert and expectant. Already his homeland Ithaca is in sight. The tension leaves him, and he falls asleep. Left to their own devices, the greedy crewmen do not trust their master and want to have a share of the treasures they believe are in the sack, so they open it. With a shattering roar, all the winds burst free and blow in all directions. Ithaca, the promised land, disappears behind the horizon. Everyone weeps over the cruel disappointment.

When the winds have blown themselves out in all directions, they quietly sneak back to their home in Aeolia, taking the ships with them. Odysseus, ashamed, asks again for help, but Aeolus is afraid to have anything more to do with anyone clearly not on friendly terms with the gods. In his present state of development there is no second chance for Odysseus.

After six days of hard rowing, they come to an arctic land, and find a rocky coast with many fjords. Eleven ships seek shelter and recklessly sail deep inland. Odysseus himself is cautious enough to stay at anchor outside, but sends a few messengers to explore. One of these men is promptly eaten by the giant king and the mountainous queen of the natives. Meanwhile their people, the Laestrygones, a tribe of giant cannibals, have arrived on the rocky cliffs high above the ships on both sides. They pound the ships with boulders and spear the sailors like fish and eat them. Eleven ships with all their men are lost.

Since Odysseus, overcome by weariness and false confidence, could not use Aeolus' help to succeed in reaching his home, he must witness his adventure with the Cyclops repeated on a larger scale. The lower forces of his physical nature, the fierce cannibals, eat, that is, absorb the half-conscious forces of his soul, except the ones nearest to him. But of those forces Polyphemus already had devoured a few earlier in his cave. This time Odysseus is able to make use of his sword. He cuts the cables, and with the fear of death upon them, Odysseus and his men strike the waters like one man and escape.

Still fearful and very cautious, Odysseus lands his single ship on the island Aeaea, without making a sound. For the second time, the Greeks sense that a god has guided them. The soldiers sit on the beach weeping and shivering while Odysseus goes exploring alone and comes upon an enormous stag. He kills it with his spear and carries it to his men for food. In a glen at the center of the wooded island lives the goddess Circe, whose father is the Sun and whose maternal grandfather is the Titan Oceanus. Like her niece Medea, she is an enchantress. She sings and weaves, but she can be unfriendly enough to turn the bodies of visitors into those of wolves and lions. The people within these animal bodies stay fully aware of their misfortune and do not behave like the animals they resemble. Half the crew of Odysseus' ship, twenty-two men, sent to reconnoiter the island, are invited by Circe to enter the palace. She feeds them a poison that makes them forget their native land; afterwards, with a touch of her wand, she changes them all into swine.

The adventure in the land of the lotus-eaters is here repeated on a larger scale. After losing the vast majority of his soul forces to lower physical processes (Cyclops and Laestrygones), Odysseus now has to fight for the clarity of his sense perceptions against the onslaught of atavistic[4] spiritual influences, the witchcraft of the Atlantean princess, a Titan's daughter. Unchecked and misused, these influences can change the consciousness of men and turn them into wild animals.

Odysseus goes to the rescue in full armor, but to overcome spiritual forces he will also need the help of spiritual beings. The god Hermes spontaneously appears and provides him with a magic herb that he is to sniff as a protective antidote. He even enhances its power by telling Odysseus its name ("moly") in the language of the gods. The god also gives him advice and directions. When Circe notices that the hero is not affected by her potion, and when he threatens her with his sword, she recognizes him as Odysseus and convinces him that he should trust her. He decides to stay with her for some time so that he can rest. At his request, his men who were turned into swine quickly are given back their human shape. The ship is hauled onto the beach, and the odyssey comes to a full halt. For an entire year Odysseus lives with the goddess, who sings with a human voice while moving her hands back and forth at her loom. She teaches Odysseus all the secrets that she weaves into her delicate fabrics and about which she sings. But these are secrets from the Atlantean past. When the year is over, his crew members (his desires) urge him to wake up to his task and continue the voyage home. He asks Circe's advice. To his dismay she sends him first to the realm of the dead, the spirit world, where he has to contact the seer Tiresias, who, though dead, has retained his consciousness. He will be able to foretell Odysseus' future. Circe herself, who belongs to a different culture, is not able to do so. She then shows him the road that leads out of this world into the realm of Hades, and explains the rituals he will have to perform there.

As a farewell gift, the goddess gives them a favorable wind. Sorely afraid of what they have been instructed to do, the crew reluctantly board the well-prepared ship and sail west for a day and a night. They arrive at the other side of the river Ocean, and land in the darkness where the dead reside. With his sword, Odysseus cuts

---

4. Atavism refers to very ancient forces operating in an era in which they no longer belong and therefore exercise negative effects.

a trench in the ground of Persephone's grove, not only as a sacrificial receptacle, but also as a boundary between him and the spirits. The dead arise, looking like ghastly corpses with gaping wounds. Odysseus steels himself to face them. His companions avert their faces while preparing the sacrificial animals. At the smell of the dark blood flowing into the trench, some of the ghosts come nearer. First come those closest to Odysseus, Elpenor, a young member of his crew killed in an accident just before they left Circe's island, then his own mother, then Tiresias. The latter he permits to drink some of the blood, and then the old seer prophesies. He tells him that the difficulties of Odysseus' homecoming are caused by the anger of the god Poseidon, father of the Cyclops, and urges him to keep a tight hand on himself and on his men, especially during the time they will be on the island of the sun. Finally he reveals that Odysseus will reestablish himself in Ithaca, and will have to travel again to the continent in order to propitiate Poseidon by spreading his cult among nonseafaring people. He also tells Odysseus that he will enjoy old age, and that death will come to him from the sea. Then, Tiresias withdraws in the dark. Next, Odysseus speaks to his mother, who tells him news of home. She speaks of his old father and of his growing son, but not of his wife's predicament. Odysseus is very sad that he cannot embrace his dear mother. Then many women, mothers, and wives of the heroes of old, twelve in all, among them Leda, Antiope, Jocasta, Phaedra, and Ariadne, come up to the trench and converse with him. As a representative of the Greek culture of the future, they provide him with historic continuity. At a certain moment Persephone drives the women away. Then men appear: first his fellow chieftains in the Trojan war, then famous heroes from the mythical past. They all tell him of their experiences. The last hero to appear is the "Power of Hercules." The mightiest of heroes himself lives among the gods on Olympus. All the spirits scatter in fear when his phantom arrives upon the scene. He tells Odysseus that it was the assistance of Athena and Hermes that enabled him to carry away Cerberus, the hound of Hades, therewith opening the gate of spirit land. Odysseus would have liked to converse much longer with the heroes, but as the dead crowded around him he became afraid that Persephone might send up some horrifying monsters. He runs with his men to the ship and sets sail.

This visit to the realm of the spirits marks the first stage of Odysseus' initiation.

Odysseus becomes subject to hallucinations, hybrid products of his own imagination, such as rise up in those who, through a beginning initiation, have disengaged themselves somewhat from the world of the senses.

When Odysseus and his men return from the netherworld, Circe warns him about such beings and tells him what measures to take to avoid the lure of illusions. On their way again, they soon approach the land of the Sirens, twin sisters, birdlike beings with women's faces and wonderful singing voices. The Sirens sit in a lugubrious meadow surrounded by piles of rotting skeletons and sing passing seafarers to their doom by promising them great happiness. Odysseus has his crewmen stop up their ears with wax, so this temptation passes their senses unnoticed. He has himself roped to the mast, the same mast that later will save his life, and listens to the pseudo-prophesies of the Sirens. He is greatly tempted, but thanks to his wise precautions, he cannot take action. The Sirens then kill themselves; the hallucinations are destroyed.

After surviving the ordeal of the unreal Sirens, Odysseus must make difficult decisions to regain the balance of his mind and choose rightly between two evils.

Circe had already told him that he would have to make the choice of either sailing between the clashing rocks, through which only the Argonauts had been able to pass unharmed (Circe had not told him that the clashing rocks were standing still, since the Argonauts had indeed overcome them), or sailing between Scylla and Charybdis. If they were to encounter Charybdis, the thundering maelstrom would demolish the ship and kill them all, so Odysseus decides to sail closely under the rock where the yelping monster Scylla lives and sacrifice a few of his men to her. With her tentacles she snatches six of them from the ship and slowly eats them up. Odysseus, as he knew from Circe, was not able to defend them.

They then sail close to the island that is the property of the Sun where seven herds of fifty cows and seven flocks of fifty sheep are guarded by the Sun's radiant daughters. Odysseus reminds his men of the warnings of both Tiresias and Circe, and suggests that they keep clear of the island altogether. The men become rebellious. Having feared death at the Sirens and at Scylla, they want a rest and no more nights at sea. Odysseus gives in, but has them solemnly swear not to touch the cattle of the Sun. When they have dropped the anchor stones, they eat, but only of the food Circe had prepared for them. In the night, Zeus sends a terrifying storm, so that at dawn they have to beach the ship and drag it into a cave for shelter. Again the men promise not to touch the sacred cows. For a whole month they are marooned on the island by unfavorable winds. They catch some fish, but not enough, and the provisions give out. Odysseus then decides to pray to the gods. He finds a spot inland where it is quiet enough for a prayer. The gods, however, cause him to fall asleep. When he comes back to his men, he smells roasting meat. In spite of all the warnings and in spite of their promise, the men have stolen from the sun god's property—a suicidal act. They see a terrible portent: the hides and the meat move like living animals, but the men keep feasting for six days in a row, stubbornly eating their sacrilegious meals. Angry at this, the sun god in heaven has threatened that henceforth he will shine only in Hades. Zeus, in response, threatens punishment. He first sends the men good weather, and they hasten to drag the ship into the water and leave the island. A dark cloud follows the doomed ship and erupts into a hurricane. The ship is demolished and all the men drown. Odysseus alone survives, floating on the mast and keel that he has lashed together. The storm subsides, but a wind springs up from the south and blows him back to Scylla and Charybdis during the night. This time he chooses Charybdis and steers in her direction. His raft is caught by the edge of the vortex next to the rock across from Scylla. He jumps up and clings to the trunk of the great fig tree that grows in a cleft of rock and spreads its branches all over Charybdis. With incredible endurance he hangs there for the rest of the day. Finally, Charybdis again spits his raft to the surface. Deadly tired, Odysseus falls down into the water next to it and climbs aboard. Fortunately, Scylla fails to notice him.

When he has passed this ordeal, he drifts at sea for nine days until he is washed ashore on the island Ogygia, where Calypso lives, another goddess with a human voice.

To continue his development Odysseus must free himself from his rebellious lower senses, i.e., his men. They have been under great stress during the last adventures: the visit to Hades, the mysterious and silent passage near the land of the Sirens, and the horror of Scylla and Charybdis. The men fear death by starvation, since Odysseus, in the process of becoming an initiate, is gradually disengaging himself from the world of the senses. When he falls asleep during his prayer to the gods and leaves them alone for a long time, they make bold to continue the contact he has

146

established with the gods, but on their own level, that of greed. They steal food from the spiritual world, and Zeus destroys them. Now, Odysseus can no longer rely on his senses for orientation in his spiritual life. He has to find his sustenance in himself, in his human condition, in his own backbone, the uprightness of his spine.[5] This orientation was already in progress when, in warding off the temptation of the Sirens, Odysseus stood straight up, roped to the mast as if it were a second spine. After the disaster, he must rely on the same mast and on the keel—the "backbone" of the ship—to support him. Carried back by these timbers to the place of choice and decision, this time he chooses Charybdis. He entrusts his raft to the vortex, while he hangs on to the trunk of the spreading fig tree (again a spinal image). To be "under the tree" is "to become initiated." We find the same expression in the saga of Buddha under the Bo tree, of Odin hanging by his hair from Yggdrasill, the world ash tree, of the mother under the Juniper tree in Grimm's fairy tale of that name, of Nathanael seen by Christ "under the fig tree," before he came to meet him (John 1:47). Odysseus is no longer inside his immersed body, but hanging over it. When his physical body, his "timbers," comes up again from the vortex, he falls down upon it, incarnating into daily life. Then the currents and winds propel him further in the voyage of his life.

At this point in Odysseus' development, his odyssey has been in progress for three years, one of which he spent on Circe's island. Having now lost all his men and possessions, he arrives alone on Ogygia where he finds the nymph Calypso, the elegant daughter of Atlas, who lives in a magnificent cavern, surrounded by trees and plants. Fragrant smoke comes out of the cavern and wafts across the island as an accompaniment to the fluid sounds of her wonderful singing. Odysseus finds an idyllic, paradisiac atmosphere. Calypso weaves with a golden shuttle and accompanies her work with songs. She is a rich Atlantean princess. Odysseus must have been struck by the similarity to what he had encountered on Circe's island, but also by the differences. Here all is quiet, refined,

---

5. It is this "spinal consciousness" which gives rise to the ancient tree images in myths. For instance, in the Edda the image of Yggdrasill, the world ash tree, and of Askr and Embla, ash and elm, the first human couple; and of Idun's tree of life, the tree with the golden apples of the Hesperides in the Hercules myth; the tree bearing the Golden Fleece in the myth of Jason; the tree of knowledge of good and evil; and the tree of life in the Hebrew story of paradise.

147

and friendly: birds sing in the trees, no wild animals roam the house or behave in ways contrary to their nature, there are no signs of magic spells. Perhaps he was even reminded of his own palace in Ithaca, where Penelope, too, liked to weave at her loom, though we are not told that she sang. Calypso receives him with joy and offers him her generous hospitality. She provides him with fine clothes, good food, and friendly entertainment. She loves him, this goddess from the past, and through her love she teaches him the secrets of an older culture, thus continuing and developing the teachings of Circe, the other Titan's daughter. While Odysseus is appreciative of her friendliness, he cannot love her, although he sometimes returns her sympathy. Though he needs these seven long years to undergo a ripening process, they weigh heavily on him. He longs to return home, not to stay on as Calypso's husband and king of this alien oceanic country, even though she intends to bestow on him immortal youth. He knows, through the words of Tiresias, that such is not his destiny in life. He needs these seven years to assimilate the traumas of his earlier trials, his experiences during the Trojan war, and during his long travels. He hopes that the time of his deliverance will soon come, and is happy when at long last he hears that the god Hermes has paid a visit and given Calypso Zeus' order to let her visitor go. Under protest, but not ungraciously, she gives in. She allows Odysseus to build a boat, shows him the right trees for the purpose, and provides him with tools, with linen for a sail, and with provisions and instructions. She also sends a friendly breeze to blow his ship in the right direction. Then she watches him disappear over the horizon, a lonely, totally independent figure, now finally on his way home, one who, however, as Zeus himself mentions, "shall have neither gods nor men to help him on his voyage in this boat made by his own hands."

The divinities Hermes and Athena cause Odysseus and Telemachus, father and son, to start moving towards each other at the same time. Telemachus is as old as the number of years his father has been away from home—twenty years. The following year he will achieve maturity by helping his father reestablish himself as king of Ithaca.

In the mythological manner of speaking, the birth of a son signifies the renewal of a hero's being. Telemachus is an "Odysseus Jr.," his father's alter ego. He mirrors the fulfillment of his father's odyssey through his initiation in the course of his own little odyssey under Athena's guidance.

In her first incognito visit the goddess Athena encourages Telemachus to act like a man. As a result, he soon dares to make the statement; "I am old enough to learn from others what has happened and to feel my own strength at last." Athena comes again, this time disguised as Mentor. She acts as his "mentor," secures a ship, takes him away from his mother, and guides him through the night eastward to the mainland. Homer describes this voyage in a wonderfully quiet and colorful way.[6] The reader has time to realize that the enumeration of all that happens during Telemachus' going away and traveling about hints at processes of maturation. They land on the Peloponnesus, motherland of his people's culture, with its center at Mycenae. Telemachus immerses himself in the world of heroes by his visit to two famous participants in the Trojan war who used to know his father: Nestor, who is so old that he seems immortal, and Menelaus, Agamemnon's brother, who has become immortal through his marriage to Helen, a daughter of Zeus. Athena and Telemachus go first to Pylos, the city of Nestor, known as a "very holy place." Here he becomes the friend of Nestor's son and daughter, the first people of his own rank and age he has ever met. Then Nestor in his old-fashioned palace tells him about the past of his people, and of the position his father held in its most important national venture, the Trojan war. He also speaks about King Agamemnon's tragic homecoming, and urges his young visitor, who looks so much like his father, to act like Orestes and kill the suitors, just as this son of Agamemnon had killed Aegisthus, his mother's paramour. Athena too had mentioned Orestes to him on an earlier occasion. On Nestor's advice, Telemachus travels to Sparta to visit Menelaus, with Nestor's son as his guide. The young travelers look with great admiration upon a magnificent royal palace. The noble King Menelaus tells them that he has learned from Proteus, the versatile water god, that Telemachus' father is longing to return home but is detained on the faraway island of Ogygia. Queen Helen, beautiful and intelligent, narrates her meeting with Odysseus, who had entered Troy in disguise during the siege. She comforts all three men with her friendliness and with magic herbs. With her farewell present, she acknowledges Telemachus' newly acquired maturity by giving him a gift for his future wife, a richly decorated robe, "shining like a

6. See: C. W. Eckert, "Initiatory in the Story of Telemachus," in *The Classical Journal*, LIX (1963)

star."

Meanwhile, the time has come for Odysseus to make his appearance in Ithaca. At her earliest opportunity, Athena goes to Sparta and invisibly urges Telemachus to return to the coast. He does so and crosses over to Ithaca, escaping the ambush laid for him by the suitors. From the way he moves and speaks we know that his travels have made him into a man. Soon he will find his father in the hut of the swineherd Eumaeus. Thereafter, Odysseus himself will complete his son's education.

Having skillfully constructed a boat in only four days, Odysseus is sent a favorable wind by Calypso, but must use all his seamanship to keep on course. He never sleeps, keeping the stars of the Big Dipper constantly to his left. On the eighteenth day, Scheria, the mountainous island of the Phaeacians, appears on the horizon. Restored in health, and well-equipped by Calypso, Odysseus continues on his way, rejoicing in the performance of his craft and his skill as a sailor. He must have been reminded of his voyage from Aeolia with all the winds in the bag, when seven years earlier he saw Ithaca rising before him and thought that from that point on he could relax—a mistake that had disastrous consequences. This time, in sight of Scheria, he stays clearly awake, but to no avail. Clouds fill the sky; darkness covers the world. The sea becomes turbulent, and enormous storm winds race in from all directions. Poseidon, coming back from a long visit to the friendly Ethiopians, has sighted him. The god is still angry at what had happened to his son Polyphemus and decides "to let Odysseus have his bellyful of trouble." Odysseus is swept overboard by an enormous wave and trapped under his boat in the water for a dangerously long time. Exhausted, he finally emerges and climbs back onto his wrecked ship. He is fearful that he may die and never make it to the shore.

Then, suddenly, he notices a seagull perched on the rail of his boat. The seagull—a sea goddess in disguise—speaks and urges him to abandon his craft, give himself over to the waters, and swim for his life. The bird hands him a veil that it carries in its beak and which, it says, will help him survive. Then it dives underwater and disappears. When, moments later, his boat is completely destroyed by the sea, Odysseus does as the gull has told him. He takes off his heavy clothing, winds the veil around his waist, and starts to swim. Poseidon, meanwhile, has gone to his palace on the bottom of the sea, leaving the hero to his misery. But Athena, who has never yet helped him while at sea, approaches Poseidon's realm. She sends

150

the winds home to sleep, so that Odysseus will be able to swim. He swims on and on for three days and two nights. Land is close by, but the breakers off the rocky coast make it impossible to come ashore. Athena gives him the idea of swimming along the coast. Soon he arrives at the mouth of a small river and, realizing that in his state of exhaustion this will be his last chance, he prays fervently to the god of the river, beseaching him to subdue the waves. The god grants his prayer, and Odysseus is able to swim inland. Totally spent, he lies down and rests. Once he has returned the goddess' veil by dropping it into the sea, he burrows for warmth under the fallen leaves in a thicket of olive trees. Athena guards him during the chilly night and helps him to "keep his seed of fire going."

Odysseus had to give up his boat, his physical vehicle, and surrender himself completely to the Protean water world, without mast or keel to suport him this time. In his swimming, he had to imitate the water spirit who came to him in messenger's disguise as a large white bird. For three days and two nights he had to keep himself afloat through his own strength and determination. The rest of the third day and a third night he slept in Athena's protection, overshadowed by her sacred olive trees. Of these two olive trees, one was wild, the other cultivated. Their branches were completely intertwined. From now on Odysseus will gradually emerge from the world of trials at sea, the wild world of Poseidon, and step over into Athena's world of culture and face the trials in his own land. The next time Odysseus will sit again under an olive tree comes when he first awakes in Ithaca, where the Phaeacians take him at the end of his visit.

The island of Scheria is the homeland of the Phaeacians, who had come there from a country close to that of the Cyclopes. The founding father of the tribe was a son of Poseidon; his wife was a daughter of the king of the giants. This heritage characterizes the Phaeacians as humans of a special kind. The gods love these people, who are in favor of peace, dance, song, and all the joys of life. The Phaeacians have magic ships, "swift like thoughts," that do not need to be steered. Like the famous Argo, the ships understand the wishes of their sailors. The Phaeacians themselves give the impression of being sea gods, and their island is out of a fairy tale, with grandiose landscapes, wonderful, well-ordered gardens, and crops and fruit that continuously ripen. Dogs of gold and silver guard the gates of the beautiful houses. We hear of a wise king and a prudent queen, good counselors, model sons and daughters,

151

beautiful slave girls, fine clothes and perfumes. This is paradise, or rather, this is Atlantis.

While Odysseus is fast asleep, protected by Athena's olive trees, the goddess herself hastens to the royal palace in Scheria and in a dream she appears to the lovely Princess Nausicaä. Athena causes her to dream of her marriage and instills in her the urge to wash all the clothes of the palace. Next morning, this washing is done by the princess and a group of happy servant girls at the mouth of the same shallow river where Odysseus lies asleep in the bushes. He is awakened by the excited cries of the girls playing ball together with their royal mistress, and he emerges from the thicket like a beast from its lair. The young princess stands her ground and confronts him. He puts himself at her mercy with an eloquence both charming and dignified. When he has washed and groomed himself, and put on the clothes Nausicaä has given him, Athena refines and enhances his appearance so that his real being shines through. In an aside, Nausicaä confides to one of the girls that she hopes he will marry her. On the way back to town Odysseus walks with the servants behind the princess in her mule cart, and is asked to wait just outside the walls in a lovely grove sacred to Athena. Nausicaä wanted to pass through the town without being hindered by the gossip that his presence would have caused among the curious citizens. In the grove, meanwhile, Odysseus prays to Athena, but the goddess does not answer.

Shortly afterwards, however, when he has left the little park and is on his way to the king's palace, Athena envelops him in a mist so that he will not be seen. Then she appears to him in the form of a young girl and guides him to the grandiose and enormous palace, instructing him how to behave inside. He is received by the royal couple with great hospitality. The good and friendly King Alcinoüs immediately suggests that this impressive stranger should become his son-in-law. Not wishing to put any pressure on Odysseus, however, the king provides him with a newly built ship and fifty-two excellent oarsmen for the voyage home to Ithaca. Meanwhile, a wonderful banquet is held, in the course of which the blind singer Demodocus tells of the Trojan war and of the fate of the Greek commanders. Odysseus is greatly moved. Games are organized, and Odysseus, when challenged, shows his mettle by hurling the largest stone disc farther than any of the Phaeacians can. Amid dancing and games of all kinds, the minstrel sings an entertaining story, which young men act out in dance. Odysseus admires the festivities, especially the dancing. Guest and hosts exchange compliments. Each of the twelve princes of the realm is asked by the king to give the guest costly presents. By sunset, Odysseus has a magnificent collection. As a prelude to what he will soon have to tell his host, Odysseus asks Demodocus to sing the story of the wooden horse. He is touched by the memories of so long ago and tears come to his eyes. At the king's request, he divulges his name. Then, gradually, he assumes the role of minstrel himself and narrates his entire odyssey up to the present moment, while the audience forgets the time.

In coming to Scheria, Odysseus lands for the third time on an island, where a wonderful princess lives who would like him to marry her. Again, she is of Atlantean descent. The islands, Aeaea (Circe), Ogygia (Calypso) and Scheria (Nausicaä) have paradisiac characteristics, and their inhabitants possess magical powers. This time, however, the situation is so light and innocent that Odysseus is not really tempted to stay. Although he has the opportunity to become a prince and later a king of this wonderful island with its great culture, he wants to finish his voyage and return home where he knows that his proper task awaits him. The island, the site of his last trial, displays all the pleasures of the world and thereby tests his determination to pursue his spiritual path. He shows his level of consciousness by telling the noblemen of the island the story of his trials and all the details of his development. They all wish him luck and sweet Nausicaä bids him farewell with great dignity and poise.

The Odyssey, Part II

When Odysseus has finished telling the story of his voyage, the friendly king suggests that each of his princely guests at the banquet give presents to the stranger who has suffered so much. In the end, he possesses more than all he had collected at Troy and afterwards lost on his journey. Next morning the ship is carefully loaded; speeches are made and sacrifices offered. In the evening Odysseus goes aboard, lies down on a clean bed and falls into a hypnotic sleep. The Phaeacian ship carries him through the night as if it had wings, unaffected by the raging winter storms. They arrive in Ithaca with the morning star. The sailors run the ship ashore near a sacred cavern, lift the sleeping Odysseus from his bed, and pile all his treasures around a nearby olive tree. The olive tree, sacred to Athena, is a good place for them, since it was Athena's impulse that had caused the Phaeacians to give him the presents. Poseidon, with Zeus' consent, later punishes the Phaeacian sailors for their interference by turning their ship into a rock off the shore of their island home.

Odysseus, meanwhile, wakes up from a very deep sleep. Everything in his homeland looks unfamilar because Athena has thrown a mist over the place. In his disorientation Odysseus turns back upon himself and carefully counts his treasures: all are there. He then realizes the trustworthiness of the Phaeacians, who brought him home as they had promised to do. At this moment, Athena appears in the form of a shepherd boy and welcomes him to his homeland. She is in a happy mood since her work is developing according to her intentions. In answer to his suspicious questioning, she assures him that he is indeed in Ithaca. Odysseus, in turn, concocts a fantastic tale about himself. But Athena laughs at his lies, reveals herself as the goddess she is, and converses with him as a friend. She again tells him where he is and speaks about his wife, Penelope, and the situation in the palace. Then she lifts the misty disguise from the landscape, and Odysseus recognizes his homeland with great emotion. She finds a place in the cavern of nymphs to hide his treasures and closes the entrance with a stone. Then they sit together by the trunk of the sacred olive tree. Odysseus realizes that without Athena's guidance he would have met with the same fate as Agamemnon when he returned home. A few weeks earlier, Athena had said as much to Telemachus, when she compared his situation to that of Orestes. Athena pledges Odysseus her help on the day of reckoning and tells him to go in disguise to his faithful swineherd Eumaeus and ask him for information about the situation in the palace. Meanwhile, she will go to Sparta to summon Telemachus. At the touch of her wand, Odysseus turns into a derelict old beggar.

During his odyssey the hero has lost everything: his men, his ships, and his Trojan booty. At the end of his odyssey, King Alcinoüs loads a new black ship with more treasures for him than he ever possessed. These he will use to help replenish his Ithacan treasury, which has been severely reduced by the suitors during their years of feasting and rowdiness. The Phaeacian treasures, however, come from an older culture, and tie the young Greek culture to the past. The ship has as many oarsmen as there are weeks in the year. It is also a new ship destined not to return from its maiden voyage. It brings Odysseus back to his point of departure, just as the fifty-two weeks of the year bring the sun back to where it started its orbit. Here an ancient layer of the complex Odysseus personage comes to the surface. In pre-Mycenaean times, before he was demoted from godlike status to that of a hero by the religion of the invaders from the North, Odysseus must have been a sun god in the Aegean area. Perhaps he sailed through the heavens in a boat like the Egyptian sun god Osiris; every day and night, but also every year, he performed an "odyssey" through the sky. Thus, a voyage by boat was natural for him.

Odysseus does not take any active part in this last episode of his voyage. Instead, the magic boat thinks for him and flies with him through the night over the waves while he lies sleeping with all the treasures he acquired around him. These images speak a clear language. At this point the poet calls him "a man wise, as gods are wise." In other words "a man introduced to the wisdom of the gods": an initiate. Shortly after his arrival, the goddess Athena appears to him in her divine form and he is strong enough to withstand this spiritual confrontation. She is his friend, and he is at ease in the presence of a goddess. They make their plans during a conversation under an olive tree, an indication again pointing to his being an initiate.

Odysseus enters his country through the back door; as an old and dirty beggar he climbs the path over the wooded hills to the place where Eumaeus lives in his strongly built hut near the well-stocked pigsties. Narrowly, he escapes attack from the four ferocious watchdogs. Eumaeus, originally a foreign prince, was captured as a boy by Phoenician pirates, bought by King Laertes, and grew up as a slave in the royal household of Ithaca, together with Odysseus' sister, who was his age. This is the hero's first reunion with someone from his past, someone who had been like a father to young Telemachus in his loneliness and who is going to provide Odysseus with a safe place to meet his son, so as to organize their joint assault upon the suitors. For a short while, he associates himself with this "warden of the royal swine," talking to him on an equal footing, as they listen to each other's life stories. Unexpectedly, Telemachus returns from his own odyssey, is greeted enthusiastically by the dogs, and is fondly kissed by Eumaeus, whom he calls "uncle." A short exploratory conversation takes place between father and son, in which Telemachus handles himself with maturity and his father, in disguise, remarks that he would gladly have been the son of somebody like Odysseus.

Then Eumaeus goes off to tell the queen of her son's safe return and to mention to her the arrival of the remarkable old stranger who is such a charming spinner of yarns and might have news from the master. Athena suddenly approaches the hut, perceptible only to Odysseus and to the dogs, who run away bristling with fear. Touching the hero with her wand, she enhances his appearance so that his real being becomes visible. Telemachus looks up and thinks that he is a god. It takes some time for him to understand that this wonderful man is his father. After an emotional reunion, they begin to plot their strategy. Their only help will come from the gods, from Zeus and Athena, but that will be sufficient. Telemachus learns that he must be strong enough and wise enough to endure seeing his father insulted and humiliated.

In the palace, meanwhile, the angry suitors again plot to kill Telemachus, whom their leader Antinoüs says, was "brought home by a spirit."

Just as Helen sent a phantom of herself to Troy while she stayed in Egypt, and Hercules was represented by a phantom in the netherworld while he lived among the gods on Olympus, so Odysseus on his expeditions always leaves a part of himself at home. That part is Eumaeus, who grew up with the hero's family. He is just what Odysseus would have been if he were merely the son of Laertes, a king and gentleman-farmer. The presence of Eumaeus, as "uncle," i.e., substitute father, provided young Telemachus with some security. Thus he has been prepared for the reunion with Odysseus. It will be a trial and a lesson for him to see his father hurt, for as "Odysseus Jr.," he shares his father's being.

In the evening, just before Eumaeus' return to the hut, Athena appears again to give the disheveled appearance of a beggar back to Odysseus. The next day, Telemachus goes to the palace and tells his mother of the interesting journey he made to the mainland. All the household admires him, for Athena has intensified his appearance, as she had his father's previously. Meanwhile, after a preparation of three days and three nights, King Odysseus is on his way to the palace after an absence of twenty years. Along the way, although insulted and even kicked by the goatherd Melanthius, he "has the hardihood to control himself." Just before he enters the palace, his old and sorely neglected hunting dog, Argus, the well-trained companion of his younger years, recognizing the voice of Odysseus, wags his tail and pricks up his ears; then, after having waited twenty years to see his master again, he suddenly falls over and dies. With interest, Odysseus looks in at Telemachus acting the young master of the house, as he presides at the table. Magnanimously, he sends his beggar-father a loaf of bread. At a hint from Athena, Odysseus makes the round of the suitors to see who they are. Everybody gives the beggar something to eat. But Antinoüs, the haughtiest of the group, berates Eumaeus for bringing such an unworthy person into their midst. Odysseus responds with a rather long speech. Antinoüs then hurls a stool, hitting Odysseus on the shoulder. Everyone is indignant. They know that "a beggar could be a god in disguise." Penelope hears about the commotion in the hall and becomes interested in the mistreated visitor. In defiance of the suitors, she descends from her rooms to hear from the stranger what he might have learned about Odysseus during his travels. She has him summoned to talk with her, but he refuses to do so before evening. A professional beggar, Irus, feeling his position endangered, challenges Odysseus and is defeated by him. Penelope, who has slept deeply in the afternoon and has been enhanced by Athena and adorned with Aphrodite's "balm of immortality," comes down the hall, where she creates a stir among the suitors. Aroused, they express their desires with lack of refinement, and present her with gifts. Telemachus displays his newly acquired maturity by telling his mother, "In my own heart I can tell right from wrong well enough. I am not the child I was." Thereupon he sends the suitors away to their own houses.

As the end of the myth draws near, Athena is busier than ever assisting and encouraging the main personages in the performance of their tasks, and sometimes putting them to the test. More than once she makes Odysseus appear as he really is. She does the same to Telemachus and Penelope. But her real work is drawing the three of them together.[7] Odysseus has been in Eumaeus' hut for three days and three nights, experiencing there a confrontation with himself in the person of his son. This again is an element of initiation. Strengthened by his experience, Odysseus now sets out to win back his wife. His status as a dirty

---

7. See: Norman Austin, *Archery at the Dark of the Moon* (Berkeley/Los Angeles/London: University of California Press, 1975).

beggar inflicts on him the pain of many humiliations and of physical abuse. Such trials teach him patience and humility. The last, nearly dormant instinct of his past as a hunter dies away in the old dog Argus. The presence of Odysseus challenges the behavior of the suitors, who reveal their true nature. By vigorously defeating the cowardly beggar, he shows that his outer appearance could be a disguise, although the suitors do not come to this conclusion. Athena makes Penelope appear to the suitors in such a manner that they all donate marriage gifts to her. Odysseus, too, is pleased with the marriage presents, which will compensate him for the wealth the suitors have stolen from his estate.

In the night, King Odysseus instructs Prince Telemachus to move all the weapons out of the house, to make sure they cannot be used by the enemy. The maids are not to see this, because twelve of them are on the suitors' side. As a precaution, Eurycleia, Odysseus' and Telemachus' nurse, a wise old woman, is asked to lock them in their quarters. While father and son are occupied with the weapons, a miraculous golden light illuminates the room. It comes from a lamp carried by invisible Athena. Telemachus is astonished, but Odysseus understands and smiles. After Telemachus had gone to bed, Odysseus stands alone in the dark hall reviewing his plans. One of the maids, Melantho, comes near and scolds him. When she has gone Odysseus has his first conversation with Penelope. She tells him of her trick at the loom: how she had promised the suitors to choose a new husband from among them as soon as she had finished weaving a shroud for her father-in-law, Laertes, and how she wove during the day and unraveled the fabric at night. Odysseus, in his turn, invents a story of being from Crete, where he claims to have entertained Odysseus. Later, he assures her that Odysseus will soon return. Peneleope likes this kind and intelligent stranger and orders Eurycleia to wash his feet. The old nurse tells him how much he resembles Odysseus. Then, amazed, she discovers a familiar scar on his leg, the consequence of a hunting accident at his grandfather's place when he was young. Pulling her close to whisper earnestly in her ear, Odysseus succeeds in persuading her not to give him away. The conversation with Penelope continues.

In the dark of night, the suitors do not know that they have been made powerless by losing their weapons and their female allies. The coming initiation sends forth its golden light for both father and son. Odysseus waits in silence and has to endure the insults of the maid Melantho ("black flower"). He admonishes her to be careful, for Odysseus' son will no longer find her behavior acceptable "since he is now as good as the master himself." In the conversation with Penelope, her former mythical status as a moon goddess shines through in the story of the fabric's waxing and waning while she is working at her loom. This characterizes her in a very special way as the counterpart of Odysseus, who formerly was a sun god. Odysseus has himself well in hand, but he causes Penelope to cry at his descriptions of her husband. Finally, he assures Penelope, the moon goddess, that Odysseus will have returned home between the waning of the old and the waxing of the new moon. During the three days when no moon will be present, Penelope will renew herself in the reunion with her husband. Eurycleia recognizes the scar, which Odysseus henceforth will use as proof of his identity. The scar also characterizes him as an initiate; receiving a scar is a final act of certain initiatory rites. Later, in the battle with the suitors, Telemachus will receive his.

In the last conversation of the day, Penelope announces that she intends to use the test of the great bow to determine whom she is going to marry.

Unable to sleep, Odysseus is angered by the behavior of some servant girls coming back from their lovers. Athena comforts him and puts him to sleep. He dreams of Penelope; she, meanwhile, dreams of Odysseus. In the morning, Melanthius brings in some goats from the farm and begins baiting Odysseus again. Then another person, Philoetius, the master herdsman, sees in the beggar a vague resemblance to Odysseus. Odysseus solemnly swears that in a few days Philoetius will see the killing of the suitors with his own eyes. Telemachus continues to behave as the master of the house. Because it is a holy day, the first of the month, the townspeople are congregating in the grove of Apollo the Archer, while in the palace the daily feasting begins. Under the gathering clouds of their doom, the suitors gradually become more dissolute and stupefied. At the table one of them throws a cowhoof at Odysseus, but he ducks out of the way. Telemachus announces that he is not going to tolerate such behavior from anyone in his house, adding, "I have learned to use my brains now and to know right from wrong: my childhood is a thing of the past." He even mentions the possibility of punishment by death. The revelers become quiet. Athena makes them befuddled and afraid. It seems to them as if the food they are eating is spattered with blood.

Odysseus is disappointed that he still has feelings (depicted as the servant girls) that are disoriented and attached to his many pseudoegos (e.g., the suitors who are trying to take his rightful place). But Athena, his "guardian angel," appears at his side without delay to assure him that the gods will help him overcome all obstacles. Penelope, who still does not dare believe her eyes, has indeed recognized him on a deeper level, for in her dreams they have met. Telemachus experiences his coming of age mostly in the fact that now he is able to determine his behavior by his own thinking.

Athena prompts Penelope to confront the suitors with the test of the great bow. She fetches the heavy weapon from the armory and cries at the sight of it. Then she brings it into the hall together with its quiver full of arrows and proclaims that she will marry the man who shows himself a match for Odysseus' handling of it. Eumaeus and Philoetius also weep at the sight of their master's bow. Telemachus prepares everything for the test. Across the higher part of the courtyard he sets up a row of twelve two-sided axes, making certain they stand with their sockets aligned.[8] Then he takes the bow in his hands and tries to string it, nearly succeeding at the fourth attempt. But Odysseus dissuades him with a casual shake of his head. The suitors are well aware that by participating in the test of the bow and the axes, they are competing with Penelope's memory of Odysseus himself, who was famous for this performance. When their first attempts are unsuccessful, they decide to treat the dried-out bow with wax. Meanwhile, outside the hall, Odysseus identifies himself to Eumaeus and Philoetius, showing his scar as proof. He assigns them their tasks in the coming execution. They are to make sure that nobody escapes. When the suitors want to postpone the trial, the old beggar asks if perhaps he might be allowed to have a try. The response is general indignation, but Penelope intervenes, stating that the experiment would be harmless, since there is no chance this beggar will make her his bride. Feeling the importance of this moment, and also concerned for his mother's safety, Telemachus becomes very serious and declares that only he has the prerogative to give or refuse the use of the bow. He asks his mother to go to her quarters and not to

---

8. In his *Odyssean Essays* L. G. Pocock offers this masterful solution to the old question, How does one shoot an arrow through a row of axes?

interfere in the duties of the master of the house. Odysseus then picks up the bow, inspects it with loving interest, and casually strings it without effort or haste. With his hand, he tests the taut string, which gives the high singing tone of a swallow. Immediately, macrocosmic Zeus echoes out of the blue sky with a thunderclap. Odysseus takes aim and with a smile shoots the arrow through all twelve ax sockets. He nods at Telemachus, who quickly takes up his own weapons and stands shoulder to shoulder with his father. At the same time, both doors swing shut and are quickly locked from the outside by the two faithful herdsmen.

Penelope takes the initiative to start the end phase. She and everyone who used to know Odysseus well, weep when they see the bow. Odysseus always left it at home when he went on an expedition. It is his substitute, his skill and willpower, his totem, which connects him with earlier mythical heroes. The person who long ago had given him the bow as a present was subsequently killed by Hercules while he was a guest in the former's house. Odysseus intends to do the same to those who feed on his provisions and are the guests of Telemachus. It is ominous that the suitors first want to sacrifice to Apollo the Archer, and ironical that Penelope says there is no danger that the beggar will claim her as his wife. Odysseus shows the suitors his signature, shooting his arrow through the sockets of all twelve axes, just as the sun shoots its arrows of light through the twelve houses of the zodiac. With this deed, everyone knows his true identity.

Odysseus sheds his rags, leaps onto the high threshold, and pours the arrows out at his feet for everyone to see. Picking them up, one by one, he starts killing the suitors one after the other. Telemachus also fells a suitor with his spear, before going to the weapon room to fetch what they will need when the supply of arrows runs out. The goatherd Melanthius sneaks out to fetch more weapons for the suitors from the storeroom, which Telemachus has left open, but Philoetius and Eumaeus quietly go after him and tie him up. Athena, appearing in the form of Mentor, is hailed by Odysseus, who recognizes her, and scolded by the suitors who do not. To test the courage of father and son, the goddess withdraws, alighting high upon the rafters in the form of a swallow. Six suitors simultaneously hurl spears against Odysseus. Athena wards them off, scattering them in all directions. Then follows a successful attack of Odysseus and Telemachus, after which Athena causes the other party to miss their mark. This time, Telemachus receives a spear scratch on his wrist. In the ensuing turmoil, Athena, high on the roof above their heads, raises her deadly aegis. The suitors scatter in panic; then all are killed. Their priest begs for his life, but is beheaded; their minstrel Phemius, and herald Medon, are spared. The women have to bring the corpses out into the courtyard and clean the tables and benches. Then the men fumigate the hall and scrape the floor. The twelve maidservants who have dishonored the house are hanged by Telemachus. Then the other women servants sobbing, embrace their master. Odysseus, too, weeps.

In the battle with the suitors, Odysseus sheds his disguise and, in collaboration with his son, Telemachus, performs his final labor, the destruction of those who have presumed to take his place. Athena's influence is everywhere. She appears as a human being, disappears as a swallow. Becoming a spirit of the air, she scatters the flying spears of the enemy and keeps those of Odysseus' party on course. She lets Telemachus acquire a battle scar on his wrist to indicate that this fight is also the final part of his initiation ritual. The fact that it is Telemachus who hangs the twelve maidservants also fits in with this ritual, which started when Athena, disguised as Mentor, took him away from his mother for his voyage to the mainland. Athena brings panic among the suitors by raising her deadly aegis above their heads. This aegis is either a shield or a mantle made from the skin of a fire-breathing monster and bearing in its center the head of the dread Medusa. By showing this frightful banner, she proves her presence in the hall and confuses the suitors, who are not prepared to fight a divinity. Also, the collaborators, Melanthius and Melantho, the two "black flowers," are killed. Finally, the house is cleansed and made ready for the new life, which starts with the reunion of the king and the queen.

Penelope never slept so soundly as she did during the night after the slaying of the suitors. In the morning she is somewhat angry at old Eurycleia for waking her and does not believe her when she says that Odysseus is back. She thinks it must have been a god that killed all those young men. She wants to see her son. Then, undecided, she pauses, and for a long time sits opposite Odysseus, not knowing how to speak to him. Telemachus, still full of enthusiasm after the fight and full of admiration for his father, is indignant at the way his mother acts and scolds her. She says she feels numb. Odysseus is preoccupied, concerned with the revenge that can be expected to follow from the families of the slain

162

noblemen. To disguise for the time being what has happened, he orders everyone to bathe and dress up and the minstrel and musicians to perform, so that the populace will think that at last Penelope has made her choice and that a wedding feast is being celebrated. After Odysseus has bathed, Athena enhances his stature and he again sets himself opposite Penelope, who has not moved from her place. They call each other "strange." Penelope suddenly tells the old housekeeper to prepare a sleeping accommodation for Odysseus in the great bed, which will have to be moved to the hall outside the master bedroom. This is the supreme test, for only two people in the world know that this cannot be done. One of the bedposts was made by Odysseus himself out of a growing olive tree which still has its roots in the ground. Odysseus expresses amazement at this suggestion, then describes in detail how he built this bed long ago. Trembling, Penelope realizes that this, in truth, is Odysseus. Crying with joy they find each other.

The next morning, Odysseus takes command of the situation in his house and sets about restoring his wealth. He tells of his plans to raid abroad and tax his people, and then there are also the gifts he received from the Phaeacians hidden on the shore. Penelope and her ladies must now stay within her room, while Odysseus, Telemachus, and the two faithful servants go out in arms to meet the families of the slain suitors.

The last trials are passed by Odysseus with great patience and intelligence. It takes a long time for him to be recognized and accepted by Penelope as her husband. But the test of the immovable bed is conclusive. Nobody else could have known its secret. The radical destruction of all his pseudoegos is the hero's ultimate purification, the last step on the path that began ten years ago with his battle against the Ciconians, where he lost the most physically oriented of his soul forces. Finally, the mutual recognition of Odysseus and Penelope brings the hero's initiation to its completion. The victorious self is united with its entelechy.

Epilogue

The poet draws our attention to the souls of the slain suitors as they enter the halls of Hades under the guidance of Hermes. Lacking dignity, the souls whine and squeak like bats. They come upon the heroes of the Trojan war, among whom Agamemnon and Achilles are holding a serious conversation. One of the suitors, hailed by Agamemnon, tells him the story of Odysseus' homecoming. Meanwhile, Odysseus visits his father, Laertes, and again proves who he is by showing his scar. He invites his father to a dinner together with Telemachus, Eumaeus, and Philoetius. Old Laertes, having taken a bath, is fortified and rejuvenated by Athena. A friendly swineherd, Dolius, the unfortunate father of the hostile brother and sister, Melanthius and Melantho, is asked to join the party. In town, rumors abound. The father of the suitor Antinoüs declares in a rousing speech, "Odysseus first lost his crews and his ships and now has killed our noblemen too." Their families want revenge. On Olympus, Zeus leaves the solution of the problem to his daughter Athena, but suggests that Odysseus should enter into a treaty. On the road where Odysseus' party is taking a stand, Athena appears in her disguise as Mentor. She helps Laertes hurl a first spear and kill his man. Then Odysseus and Telemachus join the fight. But now Athena raises an eery, inhuman cry, causing the combatants to stop in their tracks. The goddess then commands Odysseus to cease offending Zeus and bring the strife to an end. As Mentor, she then arranges the peace.

This second description of the spirit world recalls Odysseus' first visit to Hades, when the initiation that he finally would obtain through his reunion with Penelope entered its initial phase. In their answer to Agamemnon, the dead suitors again tell the story of Penelope weaving and unraveling the shroud of Laertes, at the end of which we hear that Odysseus' landing in Ithaca took place at the very moment when Penelope "had woven the great web, laundered the robe, and shown it to us gleaming like the sun and the moon." Penelope's promise will be kept: the time has come for her to remarry, but with Odysseus. The simile in the description of the shroud is a clear reference to the original divine status of both Odysseus and Penelope as sun and moon gods. The reunion of Laertes with his son and grandson restores the continuity of the family line. Odysseus shows his scar as identification; Telemachus, too, has an initiatory scar. Athena helps Laertes shed his years of misery. All three look radiantly strong. The families of the slain noblemen show that they feel their fates to be akin to that of the ships' crews. All the subjects of King Odysseus who do not assume responsibility for their deeds eventually die as he emerges as a totally self-conscious being who purges himself from his unspiritual components. Odysseus, his father, and his son quickly show their positions. But Athena's cool wisdom resolves the incipient battle. From now on peace and order will reign in Ithaca under the kingly power of Odysseus, and, in due course, of his son Telemachus.

BIBLIOGRAPHY

Allen, Thomas W. *Homer: The Origins and the Transmission.* Oxford: Clarendon Press, 1924.

Amory, Anne (Parry). "The Reunion of Odysseus and Penelope." in *Essays on the Odyssey,* ed. by C.H. Taylor, Jr. Bloomington and London: Indiana University Press, 1967.

Austin, Norman. *Archery at the Dark of the Moon.* Berkeley, Los Angeles, London: University of California Press, 1975.

Bacon, J.R. *The Voyage of the Argonauts.* London: Methuen, 1925.

Barfield, Owen. *Saving the Appearances.* London: Faber & Faber Ltd., 1957.

Basset, G. Eliot. *The Poetry of Homer.* University of California Press, 1938.

Berard, Victor. *Les Navigations d'Ulysse.* Paris: Librairie Armand Colin. (no date).

Böhme, Joachim. *Die Seele und das Ich im Homerischen Epos.* Leipzig and Berlin: 1929.

Bowra, C.M. *Heroic Poetry.* London: 1952.

Buffière, Félix. *Les Mythes d'Homère et la Pensée Grecque.* Paris: Société d'Editions "Les Belles Lettres," 1956.

Campbell, Joseph. *The Hero with the Thousand Faces.* Cleveland: World Publishing Company, 1949.

Campbell, Joseph. *The Masks of God; Occidental Mythology.* New York: Viking Press, 1964.

Carpenter, Rhys. *Folk Tale, Fiction and Saga in the Homeric Epics.* Berkeley and Los Angeles: University of California Press, 1956.

Childs, Madge. *The Other World of Myths and Fairy Tales.* New York: Vantage Press, 1972.

Clarke, Howard C. *The Art of the Odyssey.* Englewood Cliffs: Prentice-Hall, 1967.

Collis, Louise. *Memoirs of a Medieval Woman.* New York: Thomas Crowell Co., 1964.

Cottrell, Leonard. *The Bull of Minos.* New York: 1962.

Diner, Helen. *Mothers and Amazons.* New York: The Julian Press Inc., 1965.

Dirlmeier, Franz. *Die Vogelgestalt Homerischer Götter.* Heidelberg: 1967.

Dodds, E.R. *The Greeks and the Irrational.* Berkeley and Los Angeles: University of California Press, 1951.

166

Dumézil, George. *Le Problème des Centaurs*. Paris: 1967.

Dunbar, H.F. *Symbolism in Medieval Thought*. London: 1961.

Eckert, C.W. "Initiatory in the Story of Telemachus" in *The Classical Journal*, LIX (1963). (About Scarification.)

Eliade, Mircea. *Cosmos and History: The Myth of the Eternal Return*. New York: Harper and Row, 1959.

Eliade, Mircea. *Myth and Reality*. New York: Harper and Row, 1963.

Finley, John H. *Homer's Odyssey*. Harvard, 1978.

Focke, F. *Die Odyssee*. Stuttgart: 1943.

Germain, Gabriel. *Genèse de l'Odyssée*. Paris: Presses Universitaires de France, 1954.

Grant, Michael. *Myths of the Greeks and Romans*. New York: New American Library, 1962.

Graves, Robert. *The Greek Myths*. 2 vols. Baltimore: Penguin Books, 1955.

Grunelius, Elisabeth. *Early Childhood Education and the Waldorf School Plan*. Boston: Waldorf School Monographs, 1974.

Hamilton, Edith. *Mythology*. New York: New American Library, 1940.

Heard, Gerald. *The Ascent of Humanity*. New York: Harcourt, Brace & World, 1929.

Hendricks, Rhoda A. *Classical Gods and Heroes: Myths as Told by the Ancient Authors*. New York: William Morrow & Company, 1974.

Herberger, Charles F. *The Thread of Ariadne*. New York: Philosophical Library, 1972.

Heuberk, Alfred. *Der Odyssee-Dichter und die Ilias*. Erlangen: 1954.

Hiebel, Frederick. *The Gospel of Hellas*. New York: The Anthroposophical Press, 1949.

Jaeger, Werner. *Paedeia: The Ideals of Greek Culture*. New York: Oxford University Press, 1939.

James, E.O. *The Cult of the Mother Goddess*. New York: 1959.

Jung, Carl G. *Memories, Dreams, Reflections*. New York: Pantheon Books, No date.

Jung, Carl G. & Kerényi, Károly. *Essays on the Science of Mythology*. Princeton: Princeton University Press, 1949.

Kelsey, Morton T. *Myth, History and Faith: The Remythologizing of Christianity*. New York: Paulist Press, 1974.

Kerényi, Károly. *The Gods of the Greeks*. New York: Grove, 1960.

Kerényi, Károly. *The Heroes of the Greeks*. New York: Grove, 1960.

Kerényi, Károly. *Prometheus; Archetypal Image of Human Existence*. New York: Pantheon, 1963.

Kirk, G.S. *Myth, its Meaning and Function in Ancient and Other Cultures*. Cambridge, Berkeley, Los Angeles: 1970.

Kirk, G.S. *The Nature of Greek Myths*. Baltimore: Penguin Books, 1974.

Kirk, G.S. *The Songs of Homer*. Cambridge: University Press, 1962.

Lord, Albert B. *The Singer of Tales. Harvard Studies in Comparative Literature, No. 24.* Cambridge: Harvard Univ. Press, 1960.

Lüthi, Max. *Once Upon a Time. On the Nature of Fairy Tales.* Ind. Un. Press, 1970

Macpherson, Jay. *Four Ages of Man.* Toronto: The Macmillan Company of Canada, 1971.

Mattes, Wilhelm. *Odysseus bei den Phäaken.* Würzburg: 1958.

Meyer, Rudolph. *Die Weisheit der Deutschen Volksmärchen.* Stuttgart: Verlag Urachhaus, 1972.

Mylonas, George E. *Euleusis and the Eleusinian Mysteries.* Princeton: Princeton University Press, 1961.

Nichols, Marianne. *Man, Myth and Monument.* New York: William Morrow Co., 1975.

Nilsson, Martin P. *The Mynoan Mycenaean Religion.* London: 1960.

Nilsson, Martin P. *The Mycenaean Origin of Greek Mythology.* Univ. of Calif. Press, 1983.

Onians, R.B. *The Origin of European Thought.* Cambridge: 1951.

Otto, Walter Friedrich. *The Homeric Gods.* Translated by Moses Hadas. New York: Pantheon, 1954.

Page, Denys. *The Homeric Odyssey.* Oxford: Clarendon Press, 1955.

Parry, Milman. *The Making of Homeric Verse: The Collected Papers of Milman Parry.* Edited by Adam Parry. Oxford Univ. Press, 1971.

Pocock, L.G. *Odyssean Essays.* Oxford: Basil Blackwell, 1965.

Ramos, Oscar G. "La Odisea: Un Itinerario Humano" *Publicaciones del Instituto Caro y Cuervo,* Series Minor XI. Bogota: 1970.

Reinhold, Meyer. *Past and Present: The Continuity of Classical Myths.* Toronto: Hakkert, 1972.

Rose, H.J. *Gods and Heroes of the Greeks.* Cleveland: World Publishing, 1958.

Schuré, Edouard. *The Genesis of Tragedy and the Sacred Drama of Eleusis.* London: R. Steiner Publications Co., 1936.

Segal, Charles P. *The Phaeacians and the Symbolism of Odysseus' Return.* Arion 1 no. 4, 1962.

Snell, Bruno. *Discovery of the Mind.* New York: Harper, 1960.

Stahl, William Harris. *Martianus Capella and the Seven Liberal Arts.* New York: Columbia University Press, 1971.

Steiner, Rudolf. *The Apocalypse.* London: Rudolf Steiner Publishing Co., 1943.

Steiner, Rudolf. *Art in the Light of Mystery Wisdom.* New York: The Anthroposophical Press, 1935.

Steiner, Rudolf. *The Calendar of the Soul.* London: Rudolf Steiner Press, 1963.

Steiner, Rudolf. *Christianity as Mystical Fact and the Mysteries of Antiquity.* Blauvelt, N.Y.: Rudolf Steiner Publications, 1972.

Steiner, Rudolf. *Cosmic Forces in Man*. London: Rudolf Steiner Publishing Co., 1948.

Steiner, Rudolf. *Cosmology, Religion, and Philosophy*. London: Rudolf Steiner Publishing Co., 1948.

Steiner, Rudolf. *The East in the Light of the West*. New York: The Anthroposophical Press, 1940.

Steiner, Rudolf. *The Effect of Occult Development*. London: Rudolf Steiner Publishing Co., 1945.

Steiner, Rudolf. *Egyptian Myths and Mysteries*. London: Rudolf Steiner Publishing Co., 1933.

Steiner, Rudolf. *The Gospel of St. John in Relation to the Other Gospels*. London: Percy Lund Humphries & Co., 1933.

Steiner, Rudolf. *Life Between Death and Rebirth*. London: Rudolf Steiner Publishing Co., 1930.

Steiner, Rudolf. *The Mission of Folk Souls*. London: Rudolf Steiner Publishing Co., 1929.

Steiner, Rudolf. *Mystery Centers*. London: Rudolf Steiner Publishing Co., 1949.

Steiner, Rudolf. *The Spiritual Hierarchies*. London: Rudolf Steiner Publishing Co., 1931.

Steiner, Rudolf. *Spiritual Science and Medicine*. London: Rudolf Steiner Publishing Co., 1948.

Steiner, Rudolf. *Star Wisdom, Moon Religion and Sun Religion*. London: Rudolf Steiner Publishing Co., 1950.

Steiner, Rudolf. *Universe, Earth and Man*. London: Rudolf Steiner Publishing Co., 1941.

Steiner, Rudolf. *Wonders of the World*. London: Rudolf Steiner Publishing Co., 1920.

Stock, Brian. *Myth and Science in the Twelfth Century: A Study of Bernard Silvester*. Princeton: Princeton University Press, 1972.

Stockem, Beate. *Die Gestalt der Penelope in der Odyssee*. Diss. Cologne: 1955.

Stumpfe, Ortrud. *Die Heroen Griechenlands. Einübung des Denkens von Theseus bis Odysseus*. Münster: Aschendorff, 1978.

Sucher, Willy. *Isis-Sophia*. Broad Oak, Shropshire, England: Willy Sucher, 1952.

Taylor, Charles H. *The Obstacles to Odysseus' Return*. Bloomington and London: Indiana University Press, 1967.

Vivante, Paolo. *The Homeric Imagination*. Bloomington: 1970.

Ward, A.G. *The Quest for Theseus*. New York: 1970.

Wilamowitz-Moellendorff, Ulrich von. *Die Heimkehr des Odysseus*. Berlin: 1927.   1927.

INDEX

Poseidon's, 120, 144, 150
Sun god's, 146
Zeus', 23
Animals. *See also* Bird; Boar; Bull;
Deer; Sow
Chiron trained Jason in nature of,
91, 99
Circe turned humans into, 142-143
image of instincts, 10-11, 62, 87,
103, 119
influenced by Eros, 17
in Sphinx, 62
sacrificial, 144
Antaeus (giant), 80-81
Anticleia, 135
Antigone (image of emotional life
strong through suffering), 64
Antinoüs, 156-157, 164
Antiope, 125, 144. *See also* Hippolyte
Antipathy, 8, 8n. *See also* Feeling
Antlers, golden, 76
Aphrodite, 17, 20, 98, 111, 126, 157
Apocalypse, 79
Apollo
also: Dionysus, 37
the Archer, 46, 159, 161
born on Delos, 67, 121
brother (twin) of Artemis, 76
enemy of barbarism, 20
his: oracle at Delphi, 16, 39, 44, 55,
57-58, 62, 67, 111; priest, 138-
139
home in Hyperborea, 76
sacrifices to, 116
son of Zeus, 17, 20, 67, and
Titaness Leto, 67
winters in Hyperborea, 46, 76
Apples, golden, 83-84, 147n
Aquarius, 72
Aquila, 72
Arcadia, 71, 75-77. *See also* Artemis;
Boar; Deer
Archai, 16
Archangel, 13, 16-17
Archetype, archetypal, 44, 46, 54, 63,
70, 90, 109, 134
Ares, 17, 20, 99-100, 137
Argo, 93, 95, 97-100, 103-105, 151
Argolis, 111

Argonauts. *See also* Acastus; Admetus;
Argus; Augeas; Calaïs and Zetes;
Castor and Polydeuces; Hercules
and Hylas; Jason; Laertes; Oileus;
Peleus; Orpheus
and: Harpies, 96; Hercules, 76, 93,
95; King Phineas, 96; Thalus on
Crete, 104
at Symplegades, 97-98, 145
Greek heroes before Trojan war, 93
in Black Sea, 97; in Colchis, 98-100
on Lemnos, 93-94
return to Bay of Pagasae, 104-105
voyage while Theseus in Hades,
126
Argos
birthplace of Perseus (builder of
Mycenae), 39, 52-53
home of Helen (as child), 126
land of the Danai, 39n; where
Mycenae would be built later, 52
nearby was marshland of Lerna
(Hydra's home), 72
Argus, 89, 93-94, 97, 156, 158
Ariadne
daughter of Minos and Pasiphaë,
109, 119
image of Theseus' spiritualized
thinking, 122, 125; consciousness, 122
married to: Dionysus, 37, 121;
Theseus, 119, 121, 127
the very pure one, 37, 120, 122
speaking with Odysseus in Hades,
144
Aristotle, 2, 64
Arrogant, 96
Arrow, 75, 86
Art, artist, artistic, 2, 6, 15, 17, 20, 107,
133
Artemis
born on Delos, 67
changed Autonoë's only son into a
deer, 88
daughter of Zeus and Titaness Leto,
17, 67
deer with golden antlers sacred to
Artemis, 76
goddess of Arcadia, 71, 76; moon

171

Black Sea, 78-80, 89, 94-97, 103
Blind, 6, 63, 95-97, 129, 152
Blood
    of Nessus (centaur) (prompted
        Hercules' death), 85-86
    warmth (pictured as a red mantle),
        vehicle of the forces of selfhood,
        42
Bo, 147. See also Tree
Boar. See also Animals
    (Arcadian or Erymanthian) cap-
        tured by Hercules, 93
    (Caledonian) hunted by Theseus
        and Pirithoüs, 125
    image of: aggression, 75-76; in-
        stincts, 76
Boast, boastful attitude (pictured as
    waving manes and roar of lion), 51,
    68, 72
Body, physical. See also Form
    bound to it: consciousness of
        daytime, 24; soul, 24, 51
    having: nervous, metabolic,
        rhythmic systems (representing
        thinking, willing, feeling), 11n,
        71
    out of body (Odysseus over it), 147
    permeated by spiritual nature of
        man, 11, 87
    pictured as: cave, 140; dwelling
        place, 136; house, stable,
        vehicle, 75n; land-enclosed sea,
        80; ship, 94, 103, 136-137, 151
    processes of, 1n
    viewed as: machine, 3; palace and
        prison of man, 110
    weight, crushing, 19, 114
Boeotia, 55, 88
Bones, 87
Bosporus, 94-95, 97, 103
Boundary, 92
Bow, 159-161
Bowl, golden, 80-82
Boxing, 95, 98
Brain (pictured as labyrinth), 11n, 47,
    110, 120, 134. See also Thinking
Bread and wine, 34
Breath, breathing, 7-8, 87, 90. See also
    Rhythm; Feeling

Bronze, 20, 77, 104, 106, 112, 141
"Brother and Sister," 77
Brute, brutish, 98, 137
Buddha, 147
Bull. See also Animals
    disguise of: Achelous, 85; Zeus, 31,
        108-109
    image of: abdominal forces, 79;
        instincts, 85, 103, 119; sexuality,
        78, 103, 110; will, 71
    macrocosmic component of man
        (one of four), 109
    made by Hephaestus, 100; owned
        by Aeëtes, 90, 99-100, 106
    mind-bull. See Minotaur
    of: Crete, 71-72, 78-79, 108, 115;
        Marathon, 78, 109, 115, 119-
        120
    sacred to Poseidon, 95, 108, 110,
        120
Burial, 90
Burn, burning up
    of mortal parts (Hercules'), 86
    through direct contact with reality,
        47
Busiris, 80

Cabiri, 94, 95
Cadmus
    brother of Europa, 88
    father of Ino, 100
    founder (Syrian) of Thebes, 88
Calaïs and Zetes (image of man's
    spiritual forces), 93, 96-97
Caledonian boar, 125
Calypso, 134-137, 146-148, 150, 153
Cancer, 72
Cannibals, 134, 142
Capture, 11, 71, 119
Caricature, 83
Cassiopeia, 51
Castor, 68, 93, 126
Cattle, 80-82, 137, 145
Caucasus, 23-24, 83, 89-91, 97, 100,
    126
Cause and effect (pictured as relation
    between parent and child), 4, 14.
    See also Relationship; Thinking
Caution, cautious, 134, 142

173

174

Creative, creativity
force (Prometheus), 20, 24, 27, 76,
84
intellect (Daedalus), 122
nature (Titans), 18
of man resides in his spirituality, 87
power (Zeus' divine), 68
processes (pictured as Zeus'
fathering of children), 68
spirit (Prometheus), 27
thinking of: Daedalus, 120;
Odysseus, 133
Creon, 63-64
Crete. See also Argonauts; Ariadne;
Bull; Daedalus; Minos; Phaedra;
Thalus; Theseus; Zeus
Cretan-Minoan culture, 19n, 109
image of abdomen of man, 80
Crew members
image of: Jason's soul forces, 103;
Odysseus' desires, 143, and will,
136-137
Cronus, 17-19, 23
Culture, cultural. See also Athena;
Atlantean; Cretan-Minoan;
Ethiopian; Greek; Mycenaean;
Phaeacian; Spiritual; Tribal
development of different cultures,
68
disappears through materialism, 87
human culture, 17
life of: Greece, 91; tribe (pictured as
queen), 51
new stages, initiated by heroes, 38
pre-European, 90
preserved by Hera, 19
source of, is religion, 15
Cunning, 130, 139, 141
Curiosity, 23, 77, 133, 140
Cyclops (giant), 52, 134, 136, 139-
140, 142-144, 151
Cyzicus, 94

Dactyl, 7, 8
Daedalus (image of creative thinker),
107, 109-110, 119-122, 122n
Danaë, 10, 31, 39-43, 52
Danai, 39
Daughter (image of spiritually renewed

emotional life), 12, 40, 42, 64. See
also Child
Death. See also Hades (Netherworld)
angel of (Thanatos), 78
as punishment, 159, 164
at death, creative spirit freed, 27
depth of (Erebus), 17
initiation, before death, 54
of: Acrisius, 53; Aegeus, 121-122;
Antaeus, 80; Chiron, 27;
Hercules, 86; Icarus, 121, 122n;
Laius, 58; Medusa, 47; Nessus,
85; Pelias, 105; Perdix, 107;
Sirens, 145; Sphinx, 61; spirit,
140; Theseus, 127
powers of: Geryon, 81; intellectual
thinking, 110; materialism, 87;
Medusa, 52; petrifaction, 44, 48,
52; starvation, 146
Deceive, 55, 57
Decision (pictured as meeting a male
being), 11, 136, 145, 147. See also
Thinking
Deeds. See Will
Deer, with golden antlers (image of
spiritual instinct), 76, 88. See also
Animals
Deianira, 85-86
Delian League, 120n
Deliverance, 148
Delos, 67, 121
Delphi
Apollo's oracle and temple, 16, 20,
37-39, 44, 55, 57, 62-63, 70,
88, 111, 113
Dionysus' winter residence, 36-37
Demeter
creates nature's forms, 31
goddess (Olympian) of force of
growth in plants and trees, 17,
19-28
"Mother Nature," 3, 6, 28, 31
mother (by Zeus) of: Dionysus, 34-
36; Persephone, 28
mysteries (and Persephone's), 83
Demigod, 41, 68-69, 86, 109, 114,
129-130. See Achilles; Perseus;
Hercules; Theseus; Minos;
Polydeuces

176

Perseus, 51-52
Medusa, 48
power of petrifaction, 51
powerless in sleep, 103
teeth, image of aggression, lower
instinctual forces, 99-100, 103
threatening Andromeda, 51-52
Dream
inhabited by Sphinx, 61
of: Aethra, 112, 114; Nausicaä,
152; Odysseus and Penelope,
159-160; Theseus, 121
sent by: Athena, 112, 114, 152;
Dionysus, 121
Dreaming, 8, 11n, 14, 36-37, 87, 138.
See also Consciousness; Feeling
Dwelling places. See Body

Eagle (image of man's thinking), 58, 61-
62, 71, 83, 108, 109. See also
Animals; Bird
Ear, 6n
Earth
and heaven, close together (for
Greeks), 34
called also "Mother Earth," 18, 18n,
31, 84
contact with earth (his mother)
restored forces of giant Antaeus,
80
(path) deep into earth (pictured as
Hades), same as path deep into
one's self, 82
deepest realm of earth (pictured as
Tartarus): prison of defeated
Titans (creative powers under
the earth), 18-19
development, 31
disk, 80
garden of, ruled by Demeter, 28
men (earthly), 31
mineral, ruled by Hades, 19
physical, home of Gorgons, 47
physical embodiment of Titans, 18
pictured as Gaea, 17-18
on surface, Persephone lives in
spring and summer, working in
the plants, 28
under surface, in Hades realm, Per-

sephone lives in fall and winter,
keeping seeds alive, 28
Echidna, 72, 82, 113
Eckert, C. W., 149n
Edda, 53n, 147n
Education, 91, 133, 135
Effect. See Cause
Ego. See also "I"; Self
alter ego: Odysseus' (Telemachus),
148; Theseus' (Pirithoüs), 125,
127
force (of Hercules'), 70
lower ego (pseudo self), 11, 127;
Odysseus' (suitors), 160, 163;
Theseus' (Pirithoüs), 125, 127
Egotism, 88, 120, 122
Egypt, 80, 83, 109, 156
Eilithyia, 66-67
Elemental beings, 18, 28
Elements. See New
Eleusis, 16, 31, 37, 57, 83, 113, 125,
126
Elis, 71, 77
Elm, 90, 147n. See also Tree
Elpenor, 114
Elysium, 84
Embla, 90, 147n
Emotions. See Feelings, intense
Enchantress, 142. See also Magician
Encounter, encountering. See also
Meeting
animals (images of instincts), 119
bandits (humans) (image of habits of
which Theseus conscious), 119
beings (image of inner develop-
ment), 10
hero's with some aspect of his per-
sonality, 103n
human beings (image of attitudes of
which we are unaware), 11
male being (image of decision-
making forces), 11
Enlightenment, 19, 103. See also
Consciousness; Initiation
Entelechy, 163
Environment (pictured as mother), 11,
14
Envy, 107, 110. See also Feeling
Eos, 17

bride-to-be, 43; Phaeacian princes to Odysseus, 153-154, 163

robe from: Deianira to Hercules, 86; Helen to Telemachus, 149; Penelope to Laertes, 158, 164

skill and an excellent brain from Athena to Penelope, 134

tree with golden apples from Mother Earth to Zeus and Hera, 84

wind, favorable, from Circe to Odysseus, 143

wine by: Apollo's priest to Odysseus, 138; by Odysseus to Polyphemus, 139

Girdle of Hippolyte, 79

Goat (wild) (image of innate tendencies and dispositions), 140

Gods. *See also* Spiritual beings

(prior to first hierarchy) Erebus; Eros; Nyx

(first hierarchy) Gaea and Uranus (parents of monsters, giants, and Titans)

(second hierarchy) (12 Titans) Cronus; Iapetus; Mnemosyne; Oceanus; Rhea; Themis

(Titans' children and their children) Aeëtes; Atlas; Calypso; Circe; Eos; Epimetheus; Helios; Leto; nine Muses; Olympians; Prometheus; Selene; elemental beings; spirits of mountains, trees, and water

(third hierarchy) (archai; archangels; angels) Olympians: Demeter; Hades; Hera; Hestia; Poseidon; Zeus

(children of the Olympians) Aphrodite; Apollo; Ares; Artemis; Dionysus; Hebe; Hephaestus; Hermes; Persephone

Aeolus (six sons and six daughters ruling the months), wind god, 141

Cabiri on Samothrace, 94-95

contact (direct) through initiation, 16, 147

generations of, 17

loved Phaeacians, 151

man's awareness of, 15; consciousness of, dimming (Götterdämmerung), 15n, 27, 51

mouthpiece (oracle), 16

Odin, Icelandic god of breath, 90

Wotan, Germanic god of storm, 90

World of the gods, 98

Goethe, 6n

Götterdämmerung, 15n, 27, 37, 51

Gold, golden. *See also* Age; Antlers; Apples; Aura; Ball; Bowl; Diadem; Dog; Fleece; Light; Rain; Ram; Ring; Sandals; Shuttle

metalworking inaugurated by Hephaestus, 20

represented by sun's power on earth, 76

(most) spiritual element on earth, 76

Good, 23, 38, 90, 147n

Gorgons, 45-48

Graeae (birds) (image of Perseus' ununified soul; guardian of inner threshold), 45-46, 48

Grain, 34, 88-89

Grandmother (image of tribal lore, wisdom), 10n

Grape, 34

Graves, R., xi, xin

Gravity, 17, 46

Greed, greedy

Odysseus' crewmen, 141, 147

pictured as: dragon, 51; Polydectes, 43-44, 52; stepmother, 91; wolf, 40

Polyphemus, 139

senses (pictured as predatory bird), 24, 27, 147

Greek, Greeks. *See also* Education; Gods; Individualism; Invaders; Language; Myths; Philosophers; Religion; Thinking

childhood of Greek culture (Minoan), 19n

culture, 94

living around 1000 B.C., 14

preceded by Mycenaeans, 129

war against Troy, 130

goddess of: conservation, pre-
serving cultural tradition and
marriage, 19, 34-35, 68;
opposed to developments in
men's ideas and consciousness,
35
married to Zeus, 31, 84
Olympian goddess, 17
protectress of Jason, 91-94, 98
queen of heaven, 34
Heraclides, 46
Heraclitus, 13
Herald, 20. *See also* Hermes
Herbs, 149
Hercules
accompanied Argonauts, 76, 91,
93-95
asked oracle at Delphi, 70
behavior: angry, brutish, 68, 70-71,
85, 125, 161; heroic, 68
birth, 66
captured Cerberus (11th labor), 82,
100, 126
courageous, 115
death, 86
deeds reflected in Zodiac (Leo,
Aquarius, Scorpio, Taurus) 72
encountered Geryon, 45
freed Prometheus, 24, 83
great-grandson of Perseus, 68
Greeks considered themselves his
children, 86
harrassed by Hera, 67-68
helped Theseus, 82, 126, 128
helped by: Athena, 77, 82, 144;
Hermes, 82, 144; Iolaus (his
nephew), 72; Theseus, 70, 83,
125
hero (greatest Greek hero), 69, 112
initiation of, 84-85
killed: Antaeus, 80-81, 94; Bursiris,
80; dragon that guarded tree
with golden apples, 84; Geryon,
81; lion (near Thebes), 69;
Megara and their three children,
70; Nessus, 85; Queen
Hippolyte, 79; strangler snakes,
67; vulture that gnawed
Prometheus' liver, 83

labors: 1st, killed Nemean lion, 71;
2nd, killed Hydra, 72, 75; 3rd,
captured Arcadian boar, 75; 4th,
captured golden deer, 76; 5th,
chased away Stymphalian birds,
71, 77; 6th, cleaned Augeas'
stables, 77; 7th, captured the
Cretan bull, 78, 108; 8th,
captured Diomedes' carnivorous
mares, 78; 9th, captured
Hippolyte's girdle, 79; 10th,
stole Geryon's cattle, 81-82;
11th, captured Cerberus, 82,
100, 126; 12th, stole the golden
apples, 84
lost Hylas, his friend and shield
bearer, 93, 95
married to: Deianira (second wife),
85-86; Megara (first wife), 69
phantom was met by Odysseus in
Hades, 144, 156
punishment by his cousin
Eurystheus, king of Mycenae,
70. *See* labors
sacked Troy, 104
separated from ancestry, 9
served: Omphale, 86; under Jason,
91, 94-96, 99
son of Zeus and Alcmene, 66
trials of, 134
wounded Chiron, 75
wrested Alcestis from Thanatos, 78
Herdsman. *See* Cowherd; Shepherd
Heredity (pictured as father), 11. *See
also* Ancestor
Hermes
and Athena (helped Hercules and
Odysseus), 82, 148
god of: action, 45, 136; willpower,
20, 45, 54, 136
guide of souls, 48, 163
helped: Hercules, 82, 144; towards
initiation, 46, 54, 82; Nephele to
save Phrixus, 89; Odysseus, 136,
143, 148; Perseus, 45-48
herald of Hades and Zeus, 20, 45,
136, 148
son of Zeus, 17, 20
Hero. *See* Hercules; Jason; Odysseus;

Oedipus; Perseus; Theseus
image of: ideal human being, 41;
    individuality, 9, 41; ourselves, 9
Hesiod, x
Hesperides, 84, 147n
Hestia, 17, 19
Hexameter, 7-8
Hiebel, F., xi, xin, 109, 122n
Hierarchy, 13, 15-18
Hippodamia, 125, 127
Hippolyte, 79, 125. *See also* Antiope
Hippolytus, 125-127
History, historical, 133-134, 144
Homeopathic, 81
Homer, x, 7, 109, 129-130, 133, 149
Hope, 23, 27, 34. *See also* Feeling
Horse
    black horses of Hades, 32
    Fallada, speaking horse, 79
    image of judgment and thinking, 79
    man-eating mares of Diomedes
        (image of doubt), 78-79
    of: Apocalypse, 79; medieval
        knights, 79
    Pegasus (inspirer of "winged
        words"), 48, 79
    white horses of Helios, 98
    wooden horse, invented by
        Odysseus, 133, 153
House (image of physical body), 75,
    75n
Human. *See* Man
Humble, humility, 70, 134, 158
Humiliation, 134, 158
Hunter (image of cool, pure thinking),
    76-77
Hunting instinct (pictured as dog), 158
Huntress, 20. *See* Artemis
Hurricane, 146
Hybrid, 61, 110
Hydra
    descendant of Typhon and Echidna
        (supersensible being), 82, 113
    dragon with 9 heads, 72, 75
    image of abundance of Hercules'
        growing forces, 75
Hylas, 93, 95
Hyperborea, 46, 48, 76

I. *See also* Ego; Self; Spirit
    finds its mode of existence in states
        of consciousness: awake when
        thinking, adream when feeling,
        asleep when doing, 11n
    is: master of soul, 11n; it is spirit, 11n
Iapetus, 17, 19
Icarus, 110, 121, 122, 122n, 127
Iceland, 15, 53n, 90, 91
Ida, Mount, 19
Idea, ideas
    called also archetypes or forms by
        Plato, 54
    development of, Hera strongly
        opposed to, 35
    objective, impersonal, people who
        still thought in a "medieval" way
        did not yet strive for those, 2
    of Minos. To realize them, he uses
        the power from the outside
        (Daedalus), 110
    that all Greek myths are depictions
        of man's inner tendencies and
        forces, 40
Ideals, 135
Identity, spiritual (pictured as hero's
    wife), 135
Idun, 147n
Iliad, 129, 133
Ilion, 129
Illusion (pictured as Sirens), 145
Image (to be translated into concepts),
    24. *See* Absyrtus; Amycus; Animals;
    Antigone; Ariadne; Athena;
    Bandits; Bats; Beauty; Beings; Birds;
    Boar; Bull; Calaïs and Zetes; Cen-
    taurs; Children; Crew members;
    Daedalus; Daughter; Deer;
    Dionysus; Dog; Dragon; Encounter;
    Eros; Fallada; Father; Fleece;
    Giants; Geryon; Goats; Gods;
    Graeae; Grandmother; Harpies;
    Hero; Horse; House; Hunter; Hydra;
    Ino; Labyrinth; Liver; Medea;
    Medusa; Man; Minos; Minotaur;
    Mnemosyne; Mother; Myths; Name;
    Netherworld; Pandora; Pasiphaë;
    Pegasus; Perseus; Pirithoüs;
    Princess; Procrustes; Prometheus;

pictured geographically, 80
representative of: Eurystheus, 84;
    Prometheus, 24
self-knowledge guarded by Sphinx,
    62
special kind (Phaeacians), 151
word "man," 109
world of, 90
Manas (Sanskrit: mind), 109
Manes (title of leader, ancient Persia),
    109
Manitou (Algonquin: spirit), 109
Mankind. See Man
Manu (title of leader, ancient India),
    109
Marathon. See Bull of Marathon
Marriage, marry. See also Wedding
    becoming one in, 121
    dreaming of (Nausicaä), 152-153
    gifts by: Mother Earth to Zeus and
        Hera (tree with golden apples),
        83-84; Penelope's suitors, 158;
        Polydectes' friends for Danaë,
        43; Theseus to Ariadne (golden
        diadem), 119
    goddess of, Hera, 19
    mystical (image of initiation), 12
    of: Amphitryon and Alcmene, 66;
        Dionysus and Ariadne, 37, 121;
        Hades and Persephone, 34;
        Hercules and Deianira, 85-86,
        and Megara, 69; Jason and
        Medea, 99, 103, 105; king to his
        people, 122; Laius and Jocasta
        55-56; Menelaus and Helen,
        129, 149; Minos and Pasiphaë,
        108; Odysseus and Penelope,
        134, 164; Oedipus and Jocasta,
        61-62; Perseus and Andromeda,
        52; Phrixus and Chalciope, 89;
        Pirithoüs and Hippodamia, 125,
        127; Theseus and Ariadne, 119-
        121, 127, and Phaedra, 125,
        127; Zeus and Hera, 31, 84
    symbol of (pomegranate), 34
Martial arts, 91
Mass, Roman Catholic, 16
Materialism, materialistic. See also
    Matter; Petrifaction; Thinking

attitude (pictured as Polydectes), 44
becoming compulsive materialist,
    ardent collector of petrifacts,
    when falling in love with Medusa,
    48
deadly, 44, 48, 87
forces (deadly): against which a
    culture cannot defend itself
    when it loses its spiritual strength
    (then the culture disappears),
    87; of petrifaction (that destroy
    life and soul), 48
infects thinking (becoming
    intellectual) when a tribe no
    longer recognizes the superiority
    of the gods, 51-52
overcoming (ideal) (pictured as
    Perseus' deeds), xi, 48, 51
pictured as: greedy dragon, 51;
    Hades, 48; Medusa, 48;
    Polydectes, 48
Matter, material, materialize. See also
    Mineral; Materialism
becoming materialized, totally, if not
    looking at the power of matter
    (Medusa) via a mirror (Athena's
    shield) when destroying it, 47
cold, hard world of, 44
engulfed by, after Persephone
    picked a flower (comparable to
    Eve picking fruit of tree of
    knowledge), 33
essence of, Medusa power (her
    head), 44
existence (material), has hidden
    realm guarded by Medusa and
    her two sisters, 48
god of, Hades, 34
looking at directly, petrifies, 47
power of (petrifaction) (pictured as
    Medusa), 48
power over, earned by Perseus, 53
softening and opening up (Medusa's
    head gone), Pegasus can be
    born, 48
world of (pictured as Cyclops
    Polyphemus) threatened to
    devour Odysseus, 141
Maturity, maturation, 135, 149, 156

memory), 6, 7, 17
Moly, 143
Monster, monsters
  Gaea's and Uranus' first brood, 17,
    18n
  giant Polyphemus, 139
  Harpies, 96
  image of certain forces of soul, 10
  imprisoned in Tartarus by their
    father Uranus, 18; helped Zeus
    during War in Heaven, 19, 32
  Minotaur, 119
  primordial, in vicinity of Hades,
    fought by Hercules, 82, 144
  scaly, populate the spiritual waters
    of a tribe if the people no longer
    recognize the superiority of the
    gods (Götterdämmerung), 51
  sea monster, 126
  Typhon and Echidna, 113
Months, ruled by Aeolus' children, 141
Moon
  emblem of waxing and waning
    moon (Labrys), 108
  goddess: Artemis, 20; Penelope,
    159, 164
  Helen (moon), 127
  light of full moon (Theseus fought
    men on field of Ares), 100
  Selene, 17
Moral, morality, moralize, ix, 38, 133.
  See also Amoral
Mortal, 86
Mother. See also Queen; Stepmother
  Aphrodite ("Great Mother"), 20
  image of: environment, 11; family
    life, 42; present, 12, 42; social
    habits, 10n; tribal life, 10, 27, 51,
    61
  of king's children (image of mother
    of his people), 88
Mother Earth. See Earth
"Mother Holle," 61n, 76n
Mother Nature. See Demeter
Mother tongue, 10n
Motif, 81
Motions. See Will
Mount Ida, 19
Mount Oeta, 86

Mountain spirits, 18
Moving. See Will
Murder of: Absyrtus by Medea, 103;
  Dionysus by Titans, 35; husbands by
  women of Lemnos, 93; Jason's
  father and mother by Pelias, 104;
  King Laius by Oedipus, 58; Megara
  and their children by Hercules, 70;
  Perdix by Daedalus, 107, 110, 122
Murderer: Hercules, 125; Periphetes,
  112; Procrustes, 113; Odysseus'
  soldiers, 138
Muscles, 87, 137. See also Will
Muse, 6, 7, 17, 20
Music, musical, 2, 8, 67, 91, 93, 97
Musician, 20
Mycenae (city), 39n, 52-53, 68, 71, 77-
  78, 80-82, 149
Mycenaean, 39n, 40, 52-53, 82, 129-
  130, 133, 155
Myrina, 93
Mystery schools, 16, 37, 53, 83, 90, 94-
  95, 125
Mythopoetic thinking, 133, 135-136.
  See Thinking
Myths, mythical. See also Tales
  adventures, 134
  are: daydreams, 9; prehistoric
    folktales, x; wisdom in pictures,
    6, 12
  beings, 43
  connection with rhythmic system, 8
  depict: aspects of human situations,
    xi, 6, 134; human development,
    xi
  Germanic, 90
  Greek, 34, 38, 40, 117
  hero in, 9
  Icelandic, 90
  importance of, x
  landscapes, 14
  names, 9n
  no certain place, no certain time, 9;
    no moralizing, ix; no sym-
    bolization of another reality, ix
  of religion, 15, 17
  origination of, x, 15, 31, 40
  personages in, 9, 14, 39-40, 148,
    155, 157

193

evil, of carnivorous mares, 78
lust for power, 91
of: beast (bull), 78; bones and
muscles, 87; death (pictured as
Geryon), 81; giants (image of
instincts), 53; gods, 14;
Hercules' growing forces, life,
75; Jason tested by Hera, 92;
judgment and thinking (pictured
as horses), 79; language, 90; a
magician, 90; matter (pictured as
Medusa), 47-48; petrifaction,
44, 47; reality, 47; thinking and
judgment (pictured as horses),
79; will, 19; the word, 90
over: matter (Perseus), 53; the world
(ruling power) pictured as
Medusa, 43
to make everyone, out of fear, give
him what he (Polydectes) wants,
44
Practical, 110
Predatory, 24, 77, 96
Premature, 127
Presence, a, 14
Present. See Gift
Present (time)
beyond past, present, future, live the
gods, 55
form of consciousness, 13
not knowing what to do in present,
Persephone, 32-33
pictured as mother 12, 42
Priam, 129-130
Pride, 93. See also Feeling
Priest, priestess, priestly, 15-16, 130,
138
Princess. See also Andromeda;
Ariadne; Danaë; Deianira; Megara;
Nausicaä; Phaedra
image of: essence of tribal culture,
41, 52; hero's ideal spiritual self,
11, 51
Principle, eternal guiding, 24
Prison, 110
Process, 24, 27, 80, 143
Procreation, 111
Procrustes (image of conformity), 113,
114

Proem, 133
Prometheus
brother of: Atlas, 19, 84;
Epimetheus, 19
chained to Caucasus, 23-24
creative spirit, 27, 76; creator of
man, 23
helped: man by promoting man's
development, 23, stealing the
god's fire for man, 23, 31;
Olympians in their war against
Titans, 19-20, 24
helped by: Hercules and by Chiron's
sacrifice, 24, 75, 83, 126
punished by Zeus for stealing god's
fire, 23
represents: forces of creation,
development, and will, 20; mankind, 24
son of Titans Iapetus and Themis,
17, 19
thinking forward, 27
Promise
by: Aeëtes to give Jason the Golden
Fleece, 99; Aphrodite to help
Hera and Athena, 98, to give her
son Eros a golden ball, 98;
Ariadne to help Theseus, 119;
Augeas to give Hercules cattle,
77; Helios to let Hercules use his
golden bowl, 80; Hera to help
Jason, 92; Hercules to return
Cerberus, 82; Iris that the
Harpies would not return, 96;
Odysseus' men not to kill Helios'
cattle, 146; Phaeacians to bring
Odysseus home, 154; snake god
to have knowledge of good and
evil, 33; Theseus to hoist the
white sail, 116
Prophesize, prophesy. See also Clairvoyance
by Delphic oracle: to Acrisius, 40,
53; (Apollo) to Laius, 55, 58
by Tiresias to: Oedipus, 63;
Odysseus, 144
by Titaness Themis to her son
Prometheus, 23
prophetic projection inherent in all

52; bulls, 95, 120; centaur in
man, 27; Chiron, 24, 27; Busiris,
80; growing forces of youth,
111, 120; instincts, 76;
Iphigenia, 89; Phrixus, 89; ram
by Medea, 106; ram (golden) to
Zeus, 89
to: Apollo, 116, 121, 161; Athena
by Agamemnon, 137, by
Theseus, 115, 119-120; local
gods by Argonauts, 97;
Poseidon (bulls) by Jason, 95, by
Minos, 108, 110, by people,
108, 110; Zeus (golden ram), 89
Sadness, 62. *See also* Feeling
Safety, 9
Sagacity of Odysseus, 137
Samothrace, mystery school of, 16, 94-
95
Sandals, 92, 111-112, 114
Sanscrit, 109
Saronic Gulf, 111-113
Savant, 111
Satyr, 34, 121
Scar, 158-160, 162, 164
Scheria, 137, 150-153
Science, 6, 15, 20
Sciron, 113-114
Scorpio, 72
Sculpture, ix
Scylla, 134, 136, 145-146
Sea goddess in disguise, 150-151
Seagull, 150-151. *See also* Bird
Seasons, 141
Secret, 23-24, 27, 143
Seducer, 33
Seer, 96-97, 135. *See also* Clairvoy-
ance; Prophecy; Tiresias
Selene (moon), 17
Self. *See also* Ego; I
consciousness of, 15, 138, 164
development of, 40, 64, 71, 130
egotistic, lower (pictured as Poly-
dectes), 44
experience of selfhood (Oedipus'),
62
feeling of self (Achilles'), 130
human, pictured as: Dionysus, 37;
Theseus, 120

impatient (Oedipus'), 57
incarnating (Odysseus), 140, 163
individual, 11, 37, 127
knowledge of, 10, 62-63
lower egotistic, (pictured as Polydectes), 44
old, render obsolete, 12, 121
organizer of (pictured as Theseus),
120
path deep into one's self, 82
pseudo-selves or lower egos, 11
real self, 11, (pictured as Perseus)
44, 51
-reliance of: a true Athenian, 70;
Jason, 96
spiritual (pictured as princess hero
marries), 11, 37, 127
united with entelechy, 163
Semele, 35-36, 47, 88
Semidivine. *See* Demigod
Sense, senses
absorbed by instincts (taste, smell,
touch), 140
activity while we are awake
(conscious), 5, 24
behavior (typical) to steal and run,
140
-bound thinking, 77
greed of, 24, 27, 77, 140, 147
perceptions, 5, (voracity of) 97, 143
pictured as: gates in a walled city,
62; Harpies, 97; Odysseus' men,
146; predatory birds, 24, 77, 97;
Stymphalian birds, 97
ruthlessness of, 97
twelve, 140n; pictured as Odysseus'
twelve companions, 140
voracity (Hercules'), 77
world of: disengaging from when
training towards initiation, 145-
147; physical, most deeply
connected with taste, smell,
touch, 140; can understand it
intellectually only if dismembered, 106
Seraphim, 13
Seriphus, 41, 52
Serpent. *See* Snake
Servant girls (image of feeling), 160

199

determining behavior, 160
development of, x
dreamlike, 14-15, 45, 47, 133-135
egotistic (pictured as Minotaur, labyrinth), 120, 122
evolution of, 12, 130
fantasy (early Greeks' full of), 3
focused, sharp, ix
forward, creative (pictured as Prometheus), 27
god of clear thinking (Zeus), 97
goddess of, and of practical wisdom (Athena), 20, 47, 54, 77, 110, 134
gods', instrument of (Athena), 47
Greek, 3, 133
group, 2
ideas (objective, impersonal), 2
imaginative (pictured as wings attached to man), 122n
imbued with feelings, x, 3, 14
impatient, 77
in images: essential being of reality reduced to a flow of images by brain thinking, 47; modern (abstract, act as tokens or signs which label the products of thought so that they can be recalled when needed, clarity of form predominates, sound qualities vivid but more abstract, apt to be full of cliches) 4; mythical beings moved as images through people's dreamlike thinking, 14; early Greek (clarity of form not predominant, intensely colorful, dramatic, all motions or happenings in thinking were experienced as actions of thought beings, full of fantasy, imbued with feelings, not yet abstract, personified, sound qualities vivid, tribal) 3-4; images are used in production of both thoughts and language, 4; spiritual being of man awake when confronting the images of thinking, 11n; wisdom-filled activities of Mother Nature present them-

selves in images, 3, 6
in thinking: is awake the spiritual being of man, 87
intellectual, ix, 2, 52, 106, 110, 120, 122, 122n, 130, 133, 163
is: cerebral activity of man (ruled by Athena), 47; component (one of 3) of man's soul life, 2, 11n, 45, 71, 80, 83; internal conversation with one's self, 4; performed on the physical and chemical happenings in the network of [man's] nerves and brain, 11n; responsibility of man's I (his spiritual form), 11
its spiritual substance (pictured as Golden Fleece), 106
judgment (pictured as horses), 79
linear, ix
logical links. See relations
logical thinking: abstract, we commonly use today, 40; systematized by Aristotle, 2
manipulating abstract thoughts, 2
materialistic, 52
medieval way of, 2
Minotauric and non-Minotauric, 122
modern, ix, x, 2, 4
modes of, 2
mythopoetic, x, xi, 5, 8-9, 11, 14-15, 40, 51, 106, 133, 135-136
new, 62
objective, impersonal, x, 2-3, 14-15
"old-fashioned," ix
(it) out, 5
philosopher's, 2, 14-15
pictorial, ix, x, 3, 5, 14, 14n, 15, 37, 40, 45, 134-135
pictured as: birds, 71, 77; eagle, 71; horses, 47, 79; Medea, 103; sharp sword, 141
power of, 76
produced myths, religion, 14
products of [man's] thinking are: never isolated, but interconnected through diverse associations inherent in thought, qualities that guide our nonphysical

and not by others, 130

war: generation of heroes after
Argonauts, 93; Greek participants: Achilles, 129,
Agamemnon, 129, 134, 137,
Menelaus, 134, 149, Nestor,
149, Patroclus, 129, Odysseus,
129, 133-134, 136, 149, 153-
154; told by: Homer, 130,
Demodocus, 152; Trojan partic-
ipant: Hector, 129; won by the
Greeks (individuality over tribal
collectivity), 130

worshipped Athena, goddess of
cities, 137

Trust, 141

Tutor, 91

Twelve

aspects of the human situation and
one, are depicted by myths, xi

axes in Odysseus' test of the bow,
160-161

daughters of Priam, 129

labors of Hercules, 24, 70-71

maids of Odysseus on suitors' side,
158, 162

of Odysseus' men encountered
Polyphemus, 139

parts of Attica united by Theseus,
125

princes on Scheria, giving gifts to
Odysseus, 153

senses, 140, 140n

ships of Odysseus (image of physical
body), 136-137, 140

stations of Hercules' self-development, 71

Titans, 17-18

women converse with Odysseus in
Hades, 144

years needed to fulfill Hercules'
labors, 70-71

Twenty, 95, 135

Twilight of the gods, 15n, 37

Twins

Artemis and Apollo, 67

Castor and Pollux, 68

Hercules and Iphicles, 67

in mythology depict two-sided

personality, 69

Phrixus and Helle, 94

Two. See also Twins

cultures, 130

fire-breathing bulls, 99

Harpies, 96

two-headed (Orthrus), 81

Pillars of Hercules, 81

rocks (Symplegades), 97

trees (of life and of good and evil) 90

Typhon, 72, 82, 113

Unaware. See Conscious, not

Unconscious. See Conscious

Undertaking, 106

Uranus (heaven), 17, 18, 18n, 23, 31,
72

Usurper, 91

Vehicle (image of physical body), 75

Vice, 43

Viewpoints, ix, x

Violent, 137

Virtue, 43, 69

Voracity, 24, 77, 97

Vortex, 146, 147

Vulture, 23, 24, 83

Wagner, R., 15n

Waking. See Awake

War: god (Ares), 20, 91; in heaven, 19,
32; Trojan. See

Warmth

blood (pictured as red mantle),
intensity has to be maintained or
we become feverish and lose
consciousness, 42

element (one of four), 42

vehicle of forces of selfhood, 42

Warrior (rank), 47

Water, 11, 19, 77

Water spirits, 18

Way, getting one's, 134

Wealth: image of wisdom, 11; spiritual,
82

Weapon, 114

Wedding (image of initiation), 12. See
Marriage

Wednesday, 90n

208

Weight, 48
Well, 61
Well-being, feeling of, 1
West (culture of), 122
"White Snake," 116n
Whole, totality, 106
Wife (image of hero's spiritual identity), 135
Wild, 87, 127, 141
Will. *See also* Force; Power
creative will, Prometheus as Titan a being of, 20, 24
deeds of the past have as consequence our fate, 61n
divine will, outflowing power of, manifested as Titan's children, 18
free will, an act of (Oedipus' own), 62
god of action, Hermes, 20, 45, 136; supplied agile willpower to Perseus, 54
gods of will, Titans, had no clarity of contemplation, no versatility of feelings, only a constant gigantic stream of willpower, manifested as Titans' children, 18
harmoniously unified with thinking and feeling and pure in themselves, requirement for initiation, 83
is: act, acting, action, active, activity, 1, 1n, 3, 62, 83, 87; deeds, doing, 11, 11n, 33-34, 61n, 71, 137; the force in our soul of which we are least conscious, 1n, 19, 87, 137, and that is most deeply connected with the physical body, 1n; the power or energy in our soul that makes us act and that underlies and carries the motions of our limbs by which we perform our actions, 1n
mastered by man's "I," his spiritual being that is asleep (not conscious) in his will, 11, 11n
nature, forces of, never stop working in man's acts of will, 1

performed on the metabolic processes in the muscles of man's limbs, 11n, 71,
pictured as: bull, 71; Odysseus' crew members, 136-137; willful, wild, courageous son (image of spiritualized willpower), 12, 42
Wind. *See also* Air; Breath; Language
god of wind: Aëetes, Odin, Wotan, 90; Aeolus, 141
North wind, 96
Zeus' oracle in oak tree, 16
Wine, 34-36, 75, 113, 125, 138-139, 141
Winged beings (image of spiritual forces in man), 97
Wings, 121-122; attached to man (image of imagination of thinking), 122n
Wisdom, wise
Athena, goddess of practical wisdom, 20, 47, 54, 77, 110, 141
in form of images, pictures (myths), 6, 8, 12
instinctive, 76
of: Eurycleia, 158; the gods, 155; the grandmother, 10n; Jason's thinking, 103; man (pictured as meeting a rich human being), 11; man's structure and function, 87; myths, 6, 12; nature, 1, 3, 6; Nestor (prototype of human wisdom), 134; Odysseus (wisest man alive), 134, 155
Witchcraft, 104, 143
Wolf (image of greed), 40, 140, 142
Woman, women. *See also* Female
face of: Harpies, 96; Sirens, 145
first: Embla, created by Odin, 90; Pandora, created by Hephaestus, 23
image of: body-bound soul, 24; emotional life, 11, 86; the transitory, 27
killed by Hercules, 70, 79
of Lemnos, 93, 94
Word, 4, 90, 103. *See also* Language
World
Atlantean, 90